A Ballerina For Our Time
Olga Pavlova

A BALLERINA FOR OUR TIME
OLGA PAVLOVA

Karen McDonough
Foreword by Christopher Wheeldon

ISBN: 1505354943
ISBN 13: 9781505354942

To my loving husband, Chris, for his support and encouragement and our sweet son, Dillan.

Contents

Foreword ix

Preface xi

Acknowledgments xv

Chapter 1 Going for Gold 1

Chapter 2 A Different World 7

Chapter 3 Overcoming injury 17

Chapter 4 In the beginning 23

Chapter 5 Against the odds 37

Chapter 6 The Making of a Ballerina 47

Chapter 7 Starting Over 65

Chapter 8 Prima Ballerina Assoluta 73

Chapter 9 Rising star 79

Chapter 10 From China With Love 83

Chapter 11 Dreams come true 87

Chapter 12 Coming to America 95

Chapter 13 Raison d'erte 105

Foreword

"OLGA HAS A DELICACY THAT is matched by great strength and a voracious appetite for devouring space. This makes her so appealing that, at once, she can seem fragile yet explode into luxurious movement. This, for me, created an extraordinary range in her work. Her abilities to resonate emotionally onstage are extraordinary in that it comes purely through her movement qualities. There is no air biting or face pulling. She acts out every movement through her body even in abstract work. Her luxurious attack and fearlessness set her apart from other great dancers of her generation. Those Bolshoi trained dancers throw themselves into their movement. There is little that is polite, yet it is never vulgar."

Choreographer Christopher Wheeldon, October 2010.

PREFACE

IN THE PANTHEON OF RUSSIAN ballet history, there have been three famous ballerinas named *Pavlova* spanning the twentieth century; Anna Pavlova, Nadezhda Pavlova, and Olga Pavlova. Though not related to each other, these graceful women overcame struggles and hardships in different generations on their path to achieving great success and acclaim. Each entered Russia's best ballet schools, learned from great teachers who became confidants and friends, and graced the legendary stages of Moscow, St. Petersburg and around the world at different times throughout the nineteenth and twentieth centuries. Each achieved stardom in their unique way.

Anna Pavlova is the best-known ballerina of her era. She introduced the world to the beauty and splendor of Russian ballet by performing around the globe. Her name is synonymous with the role of Mikhail Fokine's *The Dying Swan*. She ran her own ballet company and lived in England before her death in 1931.

Nadezhda Pavlova rose to prominence in the 1970s and '80s as a popular Bolshoi Ballet dancer but is largely unknown in the West.

Olga Pavlova is a prima ballerina with quiet grace and great élan. She lives at a time, like Anna Pavlova did, of political turmoil. She is among the current generation of Soviet-era ballerinas to dance freely in the West. She witnessed the disintegration of the Iron Curtain in the late 1980s as her career began, and she saw the blossoming of freedom, albeit with instability and political chaos, that allowed her to travel the world.

This is Olga's inspiring story of chasing her dream of becoming a prima ballerina, rising to the top of the Russian dance world, and her journey to America, which was filled with triumphs and personal struggles. She fearlessly achieved her goal, persevered through difficult trials, and won international success.

I first met Olga in the studio of the Metropolitan Classical Ballet during a rehearsal on a steamy spring afternoon in Arlington, Texas. What I knew about her came from the ballet company's website; a modestly presented biography that contained an absolutely stunning résumé and a rather dreary photograph that underplayed Olga's remarkable beauty. She was a Bolshoi Ballet Academy graduate, an international gold medalist, and a prima ballerina, who toured the world dancing nearly every classical female role there is. How did she arrive in Dallas/Fort Worth, I wondered. Intrigued by her biography, it was obvious this prima ballerina had a great story.

When I walked into the rehearsal room on that muggy afternoon, Olga and her husband, Yevgeny Anfinogenov, who goes by Genya, were rehearsing the modernist work *Webern Pieces* with its choreographer Paul Mejia. Mejia was the company's co-artistic director with Alexander Vetrov, a former Bolshoi Ballet star, who ended up returning to the Bolshoi to coach its stars including American Ballet Theatre's David Halberg. Vetrov knew Olga well in Moscow and worked with her at the Bolshoi Theatre in the 1990s. It was Vetrov who brought Olga and Genya into the company as principals in 2003 when the couple emigrated to the United States. Though they spoke very little English when they first arrived, their onstage chemistry spoke volumes. I took a chair on the side of the spacious studio where I watched. I was riveted. Olga looked radiant, the petite brunette with soft features and almond-shaped eyes has an Audrey Hepburn-like resemblance. (*Pixie* was the word Christopher Wheeldon used to describe her when they first met.) She wore a black, long-sleeved leotard and tights. A neatly folded leopard-print scarf swept the hair off her delicate, slightly damp face. She moved with a quiet feline grace, an understated authority rooted in superb technical prowess. Her line was remarkable, shaped by her strength and flexibility. Her feet were exquisite and she knew well how to have a conversation with them.

Every once in a while, Olga stopped and whispered something to Genya in Russian, and he would make a small correction. *Webern Pieces* demands strength and flexibility and strong partnering which Genya delivered. He had a particularly difficult lift at the end of the piece that he made look smooth and effortless even while profusely sweating during rehearsal.

On a break, Olga sat quietly and rather shyly next to Mejia, who was a student of George Balanchine and Maurice Béjart. Mejia talked about his inspiration behind the piece and sprinkled into the conversation some gems of wisdom he learned years earlier from Balanchine. Olga is a rare breed who can do it all, he said, from the most demanding classical role to anything contemporary. She has a chameleon-like quality and can make herself look dramatically different from role to role. The prima ballerina spoke softly and humbly, apologizing for her less than perfect English with a pronounced Russian accent.

Inspiration led me to write her story. And only after etching the surface did I realize how deep the history of great Russian dancers is ingrained in her. Olga learned from phenomenal artists including Maya Plisetskaya, Eleanora Vlasova, Nina Osipyan, and Tatiana Popko, prima ballerinas virtually unknown to Western ballet students today but nevertheless legends of the Russian stage. These women helped Olga become the artist she is today, a dancer known for her passion, honesty, and deep desire to continually explore the fascinating language of dance. Olga is living proof a ballerina does not need to have the letters ABT, for American Ballet Theatre, or NYCB, for New York City Ballet, in front of her name in order to have a shining career or be considered one of the best of her time.

I extend my deep gratitude to Olga for the many long hours she spent sharing her moving story. *Spasibo,* thank you.

Acknowledgments

I WOULD LIKE TO SINCERELY thank the following people for their help with this book: Chris McDonough, Carol Tower, Caroline Dipping, Tatiana Pavlovitch, Nina Osipyan, Maya Plisetskaya, Eleanora Vlasova, Marina Perry, Christopher Wheeldon, Paul Mejia, Marty Sohl, Edward Casati, Sharon K. Nolan, Irakly Shanidze, Meredith Rotz, Yevgeni Anfinogenov, Valentina Pavlova, Alexander Pavlov, and Olga Pavlova.

CHAPTER 1

GOING FOR GOLD

ON A FRIGID EARLY MORNING in December 1996, an overnight train from Moscow slowly pulled into St. Petersburg's Moskovsky station. Olga Pavlova stepped off onto the platform clutching her luggage. A deep chill encircled her body, wrapping her like a frosty fur coat. She was used to the cold, but at this time of day she was typically asleep. With her grogginess and the chilled air, she stood there for a moment, as other passengers breezed by in a hurry. A little lost in thought, she questioned for a moment why she was here, which was just enough to make her nervous stomach twitch. She reminded herself that she is a ballerina, an artist. This is her whole being. Everything she does, everything she thinks about, the way she lives her life she views through the prism of her persona.

At this moment, however, she does not feel like the celebrated dancer that she has worked so hard to become, the one that Russian audiences have come to know and love. Always in her head are the nagging questions, "Am I good enough? Can I be the best?" She is confident in her finely-honed ballet technique made possible by years of serious practice. She has spent her life preparing to perform at the highest level. But there remains a small place inside of her where she feels rather ordinary.

Olga arrived in this beautiful old Russian city determined to win the top prize at an important international ballet competition. Winning the contest could propel a dancer's career almost overnight. She had been to St. Petersburg many times before to perform with professional dance companies from Moscow. But today was different. She traveled here to see how she compared with the best dancers in Russia and the world.

At her side was her private coach, Nina Osipyan, a tall, lithe blonde a few decades older who became far more than just a supporter. Osipyan had a bright twenty-year stage career as a principal dancer with Moscow Classical Ballet before she launched her second career as ballet coach. Her own rigorous training with one of the greatest Soviet-era ballerinas and teachers, Marina Semenova, gave her the clout to pass along this delicate art with authority. In Olga, Osipyan found an eager, dedicated professional, still searching for her own perfection. Osipyan spoke openly and honestly with Olga, not just about ballet but about her own life as well, and the two grew close.

Along with her for the competition were Olga's two dance partners whom she would perform with for separate numbers during the event. One of the men, Gediminas Taranda, ran Moscow's Imperial Russian Ballet. She met him when she started dancing for that company. Taranda, a dark-haired charming Svengali of Moscow's ballet scene was known by insiders for his lusty heart. He had a rather stocky build for ballet, but what he may have lacked physically, he more than made up for with supreme confidence.

Also joining her for the competition was her former stage partner, Ilya Kuznetsov, a tall, boyishly handsome blonde dancer with the same company. Kuznetsov was also Olga' ex-husband.

It all seemed quite normal for Olga to pair with her ex-husband and her current boyfriend for the competition, the Second International Maya Plisetskaya Competition. Plisetskaya is Russia's most famous twentieth-century ballerina, who once dated an American president's brother during the Cold War. Competing at this major event would make any professional nervous.

But this wasn't Olga's first international dance competition and she knew what to expect. This one, however, had personal ties. Plisetskaya founded the Imperial Russian Ballet just a few years earlier and Olga was one of her stars. At age twenty-six, Olga was one of Moscow's most talented ballerinas at the top of her career. Trained at the Bolshoi Ballet Academy, she was a principal dancer with the Imperial Russian Ballet, one of the city's finest companies. She is among a group of ballerinas today who grew up under the old Soviet system, then became professional dancers just as perestroika opened a new age of possibilities, not just in Russia but around the world.

A pretty brunette, Olga is petite yet muscular with almond-shaped eyes that give her an Audrey Hepburn-like aura. Though shy and understated off stage, onstage she portrays characters ranging from sweet to sexy to heartbreaking. Her acting range is quite remarkable. She has danced all the major classical ballets with her favorites, *Swan Lake* and *Giselle*, stories that offer a ballerina the widest dramatic and emotional landscape to cover. Olga often partnered with major Russian stars such as American Ballet Theatre's Vladimir Malahov in *Les Sylphides* and Bolshoi Ballet's Nikolai Tsiskaridze in *Sleeping Beauty*. Her *Giselle* partner, Alexei Ratmansky, went on to become one of today's most sought-after choreographers. In a crowded field of stunning Moscow ballerinas, who partnered these amazing men, Olga set herself apart.

By her mid twenties, she desired something more than just the title of principal dancer on her resume, and she knew winning a competition could open more doors. She had met Osipyan at the Imperial Russian Ballet and spent the better part of the previous year working relentlessly in the studio with her when Olga wasn't taking company class, rehearsing roles or performing. Olga's early Bolshoi Ballet Academy training differed from the Vaganova method that Osipyan learned at the Kirov Ballet Academy. Osipyan's teacher, Lidia Tyutina, danced and taught with Agrippina Vaganova, the Russian ballet teacher who branded her world-renowned style after teaching methods from the Imperial Ballet School, now called the Kirov Ballet Academy.

Like so many professional dancers and artists, Olga's onstage world and offstage life were comingled, and, by this point, growing a bit complicated. At the competition, which was held at the Mikhailovsky Theatre, formerly the St. Petersburg Mussorgsky State Academic Opera and Ballet Theatre, Olga danced two pieces with Kuznetsov, *Flower Festival in Genzano pas de deux* (the French term for a dance for *two*), and the modern and dramatic *The Last Day of Judas.*

She also performed a number with Taranda, who had become a main force in her life as her new love interest; a fiery and brilliant *Tango* set to music by the classic Argentine Tango music composer Astor Piazzolla. Osipyan coached Olga for the competition and instinctively knew their *Tango* had enough spice, expression, and technical brilliance to leave a lasting impression on the judges. Olga's dramatic flare permeates every movement. Onstage, she's a lone figure wearing a black flowing dress, and with the slow raise of an arm and the dramatic lift of a leg, she portrays a demoralized woman. Then her steps begin to quicken and, with an arched back and circling wrists, the eruption begins. Taranda, with slicked back hair, moustache, and a suit with suspenders, plays the tough guy with a Hollywood-like smoothness. He walks to Olga center stage, slowly extends his hand, pulls her in, and the two are off on a lightning-fast journey. With fast feet, he's forceful and commanding, while she's all grace and bravely keeps the tension going. Along with familiar traditional *Tango* footwork, he lifts her into overhead splits, upside down, and finishes with an onstage smacking kiss. The audience cheers wildly. During their bows, with both nearly out of breath, Taranda whispered to her, "Did you see the judges? They all stood up and applauded." Olga hardly noticed she was so caught up in the exhilaration of it all. (Later, Anna Kisselgoff, the former *New York Times* Dance Critic, said Taranada performed with "mesmerizing power as the macho partner" when they danced it for a New York City gala. Years later, Plisetskaya remembered the piece as "a masterpiece in miniature.")

When the competition was over later that night, Olga got a phone call from Taranda with the judges' results. She had won the gold medal. *First* place. She was thrilled but remained cool and didn't show much emotion. She immediately called Osipyan to share the news.

The next day at the awards ceremony and gala performance, Olga received the first place prize, a large, heavy gold medallion presented by Plisetskaya. And she danced an encore performance of the *Tango* with Taranda. This was a magical night for her. She accomplished her goal of winning gold and wanted to soak in every moment. Right away, she noticed that people around her treated her differently, like a prima ballerina.

Winning the top award came with a cash award and something much bigger. Northern Ballet Theatre, an internationally respected company, offered Olga a highly coveted dance contract. The company, the United Kingdom's top touring company, could give her major exposure in the West and launch her career in Europe and eventually America, making her known outside of Russia. This would allow her to perform around the world and there was no telling how far her career would soar.

But by now, Olga was in love with Taranda and she hadn't thought of leaving Moscow to dance abroad. Many of her colleagues had left just a few years into perestroika for careers in North America and Europe where they were finding success. Northern Ballet has been a career stepping stone for dancers from many different countries who've gone onto achieve international acclaim. Certainly this would give Olga worldwide exposure and broaden her dance opportunities.

But she was deeply involved with Taranda and her life was in Moscow. She was torn. What should she do? Would she take the career-advancing offer in England or turn it down for love?

CHAPTER 2
A DIFFERENT WORLD

By all accounts, Olga Alexandrovna Pavlova should have had an ordinary childhood. But things didn't quite work out that way.

She was born May 26, 1970 to working class parents in Moscow and raised as an only child in a comfortable apartment home in Marina Roscha, in the northeast area of the city, just a fifteen-minute drive from the famed Bolshoi Theater. She lived in the same home all her life, the very same home her father, Alexander Pavlov, grew up in. When he was fifteen, his family moved in, and today, close to sixty years later, he and his family still live there.

Pavlov works as a computer engineer, and Olga's mother, Valentina, is a copyeditor for one of Russia's largest newspapers. Her parents held the same jobs all their adult lives, and though they're in their '70s, they have no desire to consider retirement.

At age five, Olga attended kindergarten and took afterschool ice skating lessons at a nearby rink which she enjoyed. Her school was assigned to her based on where her mother worked, a standard practice under the old Soviet government. Employees of the newspaper, like all other government run institutions, were provided with free schools for their children, free healthcare and other basic services.

Because her parents both worked full time, Olga looked forward to her summers off of school when she spent more time with her family. For one month each summer, the Pavlovas vacationed in Crimea, in southern Russia. The rest of the summer Olga spent with her maternal grandparents in the village of Saltykovka, about a forty-five minute drive outside of Moscow.

The summer of 1975 in Crimea was especially memorable for Olga. Everyday, the young family spent time relaxing and playing at the ocean shore. "I always loved to dance and on the beach I pretended like I was dancing," Olga remembered. An older woman, who taught ballet, approached Valentina and insisted she take her daughter to ballet training.

That fall, Olga's mother took her to a ballet studio to enroll in lessons, but the school rejected her because she was too small. "Bring her back next year," they told Valentina. Olga was disappointed. Undaunted, Valentina took her across the street to a sports complex and enrolled her daughter in ice skating lessons. Her young life revolved around school and ice skating while her parents' lives focused on work.

All that abruptly changed one day in late December 1975. While playing at home in her bedroom, Olga was happily jumping on her bed. One moment she was in the air, the next she landed flat on her back on the mattress. Despite the seemingly cushy landing, Olga took a big gasp of air. She could not breathe for a moment and immediately she knew something was wrong. "I was very scared. At that moment, my life completely stopped."

Olga knew she had hurt her back. She doesn't remember being in any pain but something didn't feel right. Her parents rushed her to the closest children's hospital, Moscow Children's Hospital no. thirteen, where doctors x-rayed her spine. They sent her home and told the family to wait for the results. A few hours later, her parents got a call from the hospital staff instructing them to bring her back immediately. She had badly injured two vertebrae in her upper back, T7 and T8 (thoracic), were compressed and her condition was considered dangerous because she was so young and her body, of course, was still growing.

She was admitted to the hospital and though doctors treated her condition as serious, they allowed her to walk up several flights of stairs to reach the ward where she would stay for many weeks. "I remember walking up a huge set of stairs inside the hospital. I had my favorite toy with me, a stuffed animal dog. I held my dog under my arm, and I didn't cry. I thought, 'I'm strong. I don't cry.' My parents explained to me I had to stay at this hospital and do what the doctors and nurses told me to do. Just follow their directions. I was a good girl. If my parents told me I had to do something, I did it."

It's hard to fathom how scared a five-and-a-half year old would be staying at a hospital without the comfort and safety of parents. The strength and determination Olga displayed so young would help get her through what was to come. Later, it would also aid her in the physically strenuous and arduous profession of dance.

A nurse brought the Pavlovas into a large room with seven or eight beds filled with other young girls. Olga would spend the next month in this room, confined to a bed, struggling to do as the nurses and doctors asked while fighting off bouts of sadness and tears wishing she could be home with her parents. The young girl was told to lie on her back in an awkward traction position with her arms stretched over her head. She laid like this all day with the exception of a break for few hours. She would not sit upright for any length of time or walk again for a month.

Day after day while laying flat on her back, Olga's arms were stretched over her head with her wrists placed in small stirrups attached to a belt with a weight dangling behind the hospital bed. The pediatric doctors believed that keeping her in this radical and dreadful position would help her bones grow correctly and heal the spinal injury. Several times a day, a physical therapy trainer came in and put her through a series of gymnastics-like exercises that she did while in bed, with her arms out of the stirrups, to keep her muscles active.

"What I remember about the exercises was one of the movements, I had to lay on my stomach and lift up my arms and legs at the same time. Because of my flexibility, my body looked like a boat. One nurse called the other nurses and doctors over and said, 'Take a look at her. She has a back injury and she can do this.'"

For four weeks, Olga literally could not leave the room. There were no separate areas designed for physical therapy. The doctors felt the girl's condition was so precarious that she was not permitted to get out of bed for any reason. She could not even use the bathroom. She remembers the nurses changing her bedpan regularly.

"When I saw my mom, I would cry. I felt like I wanted to see her but at the same time I acted like I didn't want to see her."

Valentina was so distraught over her daughter's condition and the kind of medical attention she was receiving that she took a leave of absence from her newspaper job. She worked as a volunteer in her daughter's hospital ward doing small, non-medical jobs which allowed her to be near Olga during this time. Even today, when Valentina thinks back to this terrible period in her young daughter's life, the tears flow. So much worry filled her heart during the month-long stay at the hospital.

The accident happened just days after Christmas. Though holiday decorations still adorned the walls and ceiling of Olga's hospital ward, it didn't mask the cold chill of the room or its sterile smell. Stuck lying on her back all day, Olga remembers staring up at the ceiling for hours looking at colorful crepe paper serpentine decorations dangling from the ceiling. Under these circumstances, she grew to hate the crepe paper designs. Long after she was out of the hospital, she still couldn't bear to look at them because it reminded her of those excruciating time locked away from her family. Just the sight of serpentine designs would transport her back to that unbearable hospital bed. "For me, it was a sign of trouble." Only with the passage of time and maturity was she able to break the association of the decorations and her hospital nightmare.

Reflecting back on that period of her life, Olga says the situation made her mature quickly. "I grew up mentally as a person because I had no chance to just enjoy and play and be a child. I learned that I had to be patient and strong and I had to push myself."

Three times each day, she was required to do forty-five minutes of gymnastic exercises. The exercises she did under the care of nurses to strengthen her weakened back ironically served as a foundation for her later career. Early on she learned about daily physical discipline. And she discovered how naturally flexible her body was, something that would later help distinguish her as an outstanding ballerina.

Those first few days alone in the medical center were a hazy blur, but she eventually accepted her situation. She was able to cope with the ordeal by trying to be mentally strong and looking for something positive. "I remember one young doctor, everybody loved him. He was very nice to us because we were young girls with serious injuries."

After four weeks of traction, the doctors were confident her spine would eventually heal. But now she needed time at a rehabilitation center with daily strengthening exercise so physicians could monitor how her spine developed. She would have to undergo additional treatment to recover strength in her muscles.

After saying good-bye to Moscow Children's Hospital no. thirteen, she was sent to Rehabilitation Center no. nineteen for children in the town of Dmitrov, about forty-four miles north of Moscow. Her stay at this medical facility lasted from the end of January 1976 to the beginning of April. This time she was even further away from her parents.

The winter of 1975-76 was especially cold and snowy and the threat of influenza and other seasonal germs which could be brought into the facility was high. It was common for Alexander and Valentina and Olga's grandmother to take the two-hour train ride to visit Olga at the center only to be told they were not allowed inside. Pediatric patients were frequently quarantined out of fear of infection. This meant that Olga, who was not quite six-years-old, was kept behind glass, like a prisoner, during some visits with her family. Her mother and grandmother visited twice during the week on Valentina's days off, and her parents and grandparents came to see her on weekends. Her parents never knew what to expect on their visits. Sometimes after stepping off the train from Moscow to the medical center they encountered several feet of snow and an icy and treacherous walk up to the vast building. There was no such thing as salting or sanding the pavement after an ice or snowstorm. Her parents never knew if they would get to hold, hug and kiss their little girl or if they'd be kept back behind glass only able to see her from a distance. That prisoner-like feeling Olga experienced has never left her. "I remember seeing my mom and grandmother through the glass window and they showed me something they brought. They held up a letter that they had for me. I remember looking at them and not being able to see them up close. I was so sad."

Her first month in the rehabilitation center was spent in bed, again, and in traction but with more physical therapy sessions than at the hospital. By the second month, her doctors felt she was ready to get out of bed and learn to walk again. But first, she had to be fit with a specially made hard corset to keep her spine straight. Wearing the corset was not comfortable, but the radical procedure she had to endure to make the corset was nothing less than shocking by Western standards.

Olga was brought into a room and helped to stand on a chair underneath a rope that dangled from the ceiling. The rope had a stirrup attached. She placed her chin inside the stirrup, which was as thick as a leather belt, and stood ramrod straight with the aid of a nurse. Then the chair was pulled out from below leaving her suspended from the neck. As her small body dangled in the air, wet cloth strips were wrapped around her middle that would eventually harden into a cast mold that became the corset. "Their idea was to make the body completely stretch, to stretch my bones in a straight and relaxed position. This was their technique. I think it really worked."

Even through this indignation and pain, Olga did as her doctors ordered. She wore the corset during the day while learning to walk again. It took several days to regain the strength in her legs and a couple days just to get out of bed and take a few steps. Many visits with her mother were spent on walks around the compound with Olga hugging the wall for support. For a time afterward, using the stairs meant walking slowly sideways down and up the steps.

By now, her daily gymnastic classes were with groups of other young patients at the center and the difficulty increased. The children wore one-pound arm and ankle weights and this time these exercises were set to music. Massage was also an integral part of her therapy as well as swimming. She learned to swim, by doctor's orders, at the center's large pool. When her treatment was complete and it was time to go home, doctors reviewed her condition with her parents. Under no circumstances could she resume ice skating, it was simply too dangerous for a young girl recovering from a spinal injury. "I wasn't allowed to ice skate or ride a bicycle, and they told me, 'When you play with other children be careful.' I don't remember being around a lot of other children. Most of the time I was with my parents, I was under their control."

The injury forced Olga to learn how to push herself physically at a young age. While most kids her age enjoyed playtime, she was learning how to physically work with her body and use her muscles to build her strength. Her unfortunate accident actually laid a foundation to build her mental and physical strength that would later be needed to pursue her dream.

Olga left the rehab center with instructions to continue the gymnastics at home, a soft fabric corset she would still wear at night, and the determination to press through a difficult situation. The corset had long ribbons attached. At night, Valentina tied them around Olga's bed to strap her in so she could not move about. This went on for several months until the following summer when she returned to see her original doctor at the children's hospital. By then, she no longer needed the corset and her back healed normally. The physician's final recommendation would be the most joyful one to Olga. She suggested ballet lessons to strengthen the child's muscles.

Valentina wasted no time signing up her daughter, now six, for ballet. She was so relieved Olga was finally home and taking ballet lessons to improve her physical strength. In September 1976, Valentina took Olga back to the first ballet school that rejected her small daughter a year earlier. This time she was admitted and her first instructor was Tamara Varlamova, a former first soloist with the Bolshoi Ballet. Aside from the woman on the beach, who spotted Olga the year before, this was the first professional ballerina who recognized the potential in young Olga. Varlamova told Valentina that her daughter had great feet for dancing and to keep developing her.

Olga remembers a few things about those first ballet lessons, a few snapshots in her head about what she felt in her first class.

"I remember the wall in front of me and the barre. And they taught us to do plié and battement tendu. I remember demi-plié, battement degage. I felt like I really wanted to learn that and make it real nice. It was an unusual position for us, turnout. It's kind of difficult to push yourself and let your body get this feeling. You have to be really patient, otherwise you quit and you'll never learn."

That fall as a celebration of Olga's improved health and the beginning of ballet, her parents took her to the Bolshoi Ballet Theater for a performance of *Swan Lake*. If Valentina was trying to whet her daughter's appetite for ballet and make her fall in love with the art, she could not have chosen a better story ballet than this. Somewhere in her heart, she dreamed that her daughter would one day dance the role of the main character Odette/Odile and believed it would be possible.

The Bolshoi Ballet Theater's 1976 performance of Yuri Grigorovich's *Swan Lake* starred Ludmila Semenyaka, an impeccable ballerina who studied at the Vaganova School in St. Petersburg and performed with the Kirov Ballet before coming to the Bolshoi at age twenty in 1972.

Olga sat in the audience with her parents and was mesmerized by Semenyaka's dazzling performance and the entire production. "We were sitting higher than the orchestra pit on the first or second level and in the center. I don't remember much about the theater but I remember seeing the stage in front of me and feeling, 'Ah.' It was wonderful. And it amazed me. It's hard to describe really, you're so excited and inspired watching the performance and interested in everything that's happening onstage and everything with the music and the beautiful costumes and the light. They showed me a different world."

This was the first live ballet performance Olga had seen and it left an indelible impression on her. She was dazzled and transformed watching the show and somehow carried away by the music, especially its Act III, the famous *Black Swan pas de deux*, which years later would become a signature role for her. She came away wanting desperately to become a ballerina.

"The idea of music and painted stage sets and costumes and lighting and choreography together with the ballet movements creates some kind of magic. I just

remember the whole picture, the whole story, everything came together magically. It's not possible to see anything the same, to get the same feeling in life. I wanted to learn much more. And I wanted to do the same thing."

Most ballet lovers are impressed by *Swan Lake's* Act III where the Black Swan's 32 fouetté turns create a frenzy of audience cheer. But for Olga, the drama that unfolded between the characters, where each of Prince Siegfried's would-be brides present themselves to him at the ball, spoke to her on a deeper level. "I was impressed by the magic and harmony of the connection between the music and the movements and how everything came together."

She had seen many ballet performances on television because the Soviet government spent a lot of money on the arts and showed its citizens the country's rich cultural heritage. But nothing could compare with seeing a live performance. Sitting in the theater brought the art of ballet alive for her and she wanted desperately to become a part of it.

As Olga was becoming enchanted with ballet, the young girl could hardly know of the political conditions surrounding her that resulted in the defections of many of her country's top ballet dancers including Rudolf Nureyev, Natalia Makarova, and Mikhail Baryshnikov. The Soviet Union borders remained closed and its people still lived isolated from the West, and inside, Russian defectors were never mentioned, as Baryshnikov discovered as a Vaganova Ballet Academy student. His close mentor and instructor Alexander Pushkin never talked about his former student, Rudolf Nureyev, until Baryshnikov saw a photo of Nureyev at Pushkin's home and asked who he was.

It certainly seemed unimaginable at the time that the Iron Curtain would eventually crumble and the Soviet Union would cease to exist as the world knew it.

CHAPTER 3
OVERCOMING INJURY

As Olga celebrated her ninth birthday, she had much to be thankful for. Her spinal injury was behind her, for the most part, and she was well on her way, at least in her own mind, to fulfilling her dream of becoming a ballerina.

In ballet school, she was excelling faster than most of the other young girls, because she learned early on how to push herself through demanding workouts and because she fell in love with the art of ballet and desperately wanted to learn its language. In class, she drew upon a reservoir of stamina and sheer determination she learned as a young patient in the hospital. Now with her goal clear, she wasn't going to let anything stop her. Unfazed by the constant reminders from her mother and teachers of the hard work needed to reach her goal, Olga pressed on with her dream.

Although her back seemed fine, doctors still monitored her progress. Valentina was determined to find the best physicians in Moscow to provide continuing supervisory care for her daughter. Worried the spinal injury could prevent Olga from fulfilling her dream, Valentina pursued every connection she had to accomplish this. Through her newspaper job, Valentina had met the famous Russian physician Xenia Vincentini, the first wife of the Soviet Union's most important and mysterious rocket scientist of the twentieth century, Sergey Korolyov. Dr. Vincentini was an orthopedic consultant on matters for the newspaper and Valentina asked her to see Olga.

After the medical evaluation, Valentina pleaded with Dr. Vincentini to help get Olga into the Central Institute for Traumatology and Orthopaedics, Moscow's premiere medical facility at the time for children with back and spinal injuries. The center made international news in the 1960s and '70s for treating famous Soviets who had been injured including Olympiad Valeri Brumel and gymnast Elena Mukhina among other sports greats.

Dr. Vincentini consented and wrote a letter recommending Olga as a patient of the center. This would be the only way Olga could be seen by doctors there. The Pavlovas received health care through Valentina's employer, but she knew those physicians were not specialists in sports medicine, and she felt it was essential her daughter receive expert care if she were to progress in the uber-competitive world of Russian ballet. Valentina was relieved her daughter would get the best care available.

Olga regularly went to the Central Institute for Traumatology and Orthopaedics for check ups and x-rays. Doctors told Valentina not to worry about the past injury and let her daughter enjoy her childhood. They also advised Olga to continue with gymnastic exercises to strengthen her back and to stay active and not sit around the house. The Pavlovas knew how grim the situation could be. Without a letter from a reputable doctor stating that Olga was fit to dance, despite an *s*-curve that had subsequently developed in her spine, she would not be accepted into a major ballet school like the Bolshoi.

Olga's dancing dreams began after seeing *Swan Lake* at the lavish Bolshoi Theatre. Even though she grew up in the shadow of that world-renowned theater, she didn't take it for granted. She felt privileged to live close to such a great Russian institution and desperately wanted to attend its school and learn from the legends she regularly watched perform classical Russian ballet on television.

In the late spring of 1979, Alexander and Valentina applied for their daughter to attend the Bolshoi Ballet Academy. They received a letter explaining that Olga was eligible to audition during a two-day selection period for a one-year preparatory program but not for the academy itself.

Walking into audition on the first day at the Bolshoi Ballet Academy building, Olga was nervous. Some of Moscow's best ballet dancers who were now Bolshoi instructors served as the judges. This was also her first meeting with the infamous head of the Bolshoi Ballet Academy, Sofia Nikolaevna Golovkina, whom the *New York Times* described in their 2004 obituary of her as "an assertive representative of Soviet-era ballet." Golovkina ran the school with a tight grip for forty years and earned an international reputation for turning out award-winning prima ballerinas and some of the world's best male dancers.

"There was a huge lobby filled with many parents and children and they took groups in and brought them out and they said who passed and who didn't," Olga remembered. They checked for proper body alignment and placement in each dancer; the straightness of their back, the arch of their feet and how high they could jump. They were also tested on their ability to learn the ballet language and how they listened to music. "They gave us a tempo like, one, two, one two three, and we had to repeat it to make sure we knew the difference. There was a large room and there was a judge and the director of the academy. I was scared of her all the time. She made the decisions who would dance and who would leave."

She was one of about 100 girls in her group vying for a spot. Among them, she was the only one accepted into the prestigious program. It would not be the last time she won the favor of ballet greats. She was instructed to come back the next day for a medical evaluation.

The first floor of the massive school houses medical offices. This is where doctors examined Olga's back, discovering a curvature of her spine. Valentina told them Olga had special written permission from the Central Institute of Traumatology and Orthopaedics stating she was fit to dance. But doctors wanted more time to weigh her case, and Olga left the school not knowing her fate. Several months passed before the young girl received a letter of acceptance into the Bolshoi Ballet Academy's one-year preparatory program. She was elated but her parents remained cautious, wondering if their daughter would remain injury-free and if their doctors would continue to allow her to dance.

That autumn, Olga started the program and worked hard, determined to demonstrate her commitment and advance. The teachers were rigid and discipline was strictly enforced. At the end of the program in the spring, the students competed against each other during three days of tryouts for acceptance into the prestigious Bolshoi Ballet Academy.

It was a tiring year for Olga. She worked hard at the school, pushing herself to learn new ballet steps and perfect the ones she already learned as well as keep up with her academic studies. At home she didn't rest much, continuing the gymnastics exercises her doctors had prescribed years before. Russian rhythmic gymnastics helps build muscle strength, flexibility, and extensions. The added exercise gave Olga a physical advantage over her peers many of whom would not be selected to advance to the academy. Yet, as much as she wanted to earn a spot in the academy, she had to contend with the real fear the Bolshoi's doctors might deem her ineligible to continue because of her curved spine. She worried constantly that her dream of dancing professionally might be cut short at any moment.

On the first day of the tryout, students showed Golovkina dance combinations they learned earlier that year and performed an improvisational dance. On the second day, each student was interviewed alone, without their parents, about their desire to dance professionally. Olga remembers being asked why she wanted to pursue a ballet career. She answered, quite simply, that dancing was her passion and she could not imagine wanting anything more than a life filled with dance. On the final day of the tryout, students endured an extensive physical evaluation, this one more probing than the last. Doctors examined the dancers' bones, muscles, and eyes and charted their weight, height, and feet. Doctors also checked youngsters' heartbeats and measured the length of their necks. The Bolshoi's ideal dancer has a long neck, small head, and long lean limbs. Olga and her classmates would have to get used to this intense medical scrutiny. The examination was given each year to document a dancer's growth.

When it came to the spine exam, doctors at the school, again, warned Valentina that Olga's *s*-curve could be a problem. Valentina reiterated that Olga's personal physicians were aware of the problem and performed x-rays every six months to monitor the condition.

Olga passed on every level and was admitted into her dream school at age ten.

But over the next eight years, trying to reach graduation would prove harder than imagined and she would come to learn that the making of a ballerina does not come without a price.

CHAPTER 4
IN THE BEGINNING

SEPTEMBER 1, 1980, MARKED THE first day of class for Olga at the Bolshoi Ballet Academy. What was going on outside her world, not more than a short car drive away, would later affect her career and the lives of every Soviet citizen. The Cold War still dominated international relations with the global super powers, and the Soviet Union stood as one country with Leonid Brezhnev ruling its Communist Party with an iron fist.

The great fall of the Iron Curtain was still several years away and government reforms under Soviet leader Mikhail Gorbachev further away still. The break up of the Soviet Union and the introduction of capitalism would have an enormous effect on its citizens. Perestroika, Gorbachev's economic and political reforms that began in 1986, would change the direction of Russian ballet unlike anything else.

At age ten, Olga joined a select group of young girls and boys in the Bolshoi's prestigious dance program. Her goal was to graduate from the academy which meant guaranteed placement with a top ballet company, possibly the Bolshoi itself, a steady income, and a certain level of fame that accompanied it in Russia. The Bolshoi Ballet Academy is known in Russia as the Moscow State Academy of Choreography and has a long and storied past beginning 242 years ago.

Annual school exams weeded out many students who did not have what it took for a professional ballet career. The academy was famous for its rigorous dance instruction and academics, and it drew aspiring students from Moscow, elsewhere in Russia, and other countries as well.

Nervous and anxious students performed at end-of-the-year exams for the school's top instructors and its draconian artistic director Golovkina. "Everything depended on her decision and that of a judge during examination," Olga said. "If the other instructors said, 'Yes,' and she said, 'No,' it was no. She was an extremely powerful person in the ballet world. She had enormous influence. She chose what kind of life people would have."

For Olga, the real test came at the end of her fifth year. The final three years until graduation were the most competitive. During this time, students worked even more closely with their teachers, most of whom were former Bolshoi and Kirov Ballet dancers. While some instructors didn't necessarily have long careers onstage, or star charisma for the theater, they had technical and artistic excellence and the devotion to teach.

Since Olga already lived in Moscow, she took the subway to school each day with her mother accompanying her. The academy, an enormous three-story building in the southwest area of the city, was about a twenty-minute ride from the Bolshoi Theater. The academy is the training center for the Bolshoi Ballet, although many students go onto other ballet companies, similar to how the School of American Ballet supplies dancers for the New York City Ballet.

Most of the students were from Moscow, but those who came from other regions of Russia and other countries, including one boy from the United States, lived in the dorms.

Each morning Olga entered the front lobby to start class at 9 a.m. There was a separate entrance on the other side of the building for dormitory students who lived on the third floor. The first floor housed administrative offices, doctors' offices, the cafeteria, a large gymnastics studio, a costume storage area, and a large auditorium for classes.

The second floor was dedicated to ballet studios, about twenty in all, which were surrounded by an open courtyard. There were also large dressing rooms for students to change in; four for girls, four for boys. The third floor housed academic classrooms, piano studios, and the dormitory.

School days were packed with dance and academic classes. Students were kept busy, running up and down the stairs to classes on each floor, with two hours of training in pure, classical ballet and lots of memorization of the French names of positions and steps. This was followed by classes in breathing technique, music and rhythm structure, historical dance, (character dance, partnering, and acting were later added) and gymnastics. Academics included math, biology, chemistry, geography, anatomy, Russian and French languages, history, and piano. Saturdays were more of the same. Sunday was the only day students had to rest.

Girls were required to wear drab uniforms; a dark brown dress with a black or white apron and white collar and cuffs. Boys wore a white shirt and blue pants and jacket. Uniforms were mandatory until age fifteen.

Olga's first and second year teacher, Irina Nikolaevna Dashkova, was a former Bolshoi ballerina who epitomized prima ballerina beauty and elegance. Dashkova wore high heels when she taught, as did other former ballerinas, and always looked the part of a graceful ballerina even though she had not danced onstage in years. She wore beautiful makeup and moved effortlessly around the studio in her heels. Her fluid line and exquisitely arched feet left her young students in awe.

Her students called her Irina Nicolaevna, her first and middle name, a uniquely Russian custom and show of respect. Russian middle names are taken from the father's first name.

Dashkova was tough but fair. She steeped her students in the basic fundamentals of ballet and had them keep a journal filled with copious notes on the French words for the steps and moves, and sketches of the correct body movements. She taught them to envision each movement as a different color in an attempt to awaken their imagination and to make each motion natural for the audience. For instance, *grand battement* with the proper body alignment and *épaulement* should be thought of as holding a book away from the body while reading it. She also had each student write a long list of areas to work on in their practice routines during their summers off.

Dashkova saw talent in Olga, but also noticed she strove for perfection and was afraid to make mistakes. She was also the first instructor who pointed out that Olga's muscular legs could hinder an onstage career. Yet she also assured Olga that she could sculpt her muscles to change their appearance through hard work. She was taught how to strengthen her muscles for correct ballet technique without overdeveloping them and making them look unfeminine.

Another teacher in the school, Vera Kulikova, who taught only boys at the time, often observed the girls classes and came to know Olga well. Girls and boys were taught together except for ballet technique, which they learned separately. Eager to absorb as much as she could, Olga was inquisitive about everything. "You ask lots of good questions," Kulikova told Olga. "You don't just repeat what the teacher says but you ask why. You'll make a good teacher some day."

While the first year was filled with the basic foundations, pointe was introduced in the second, when most girls were eleven. The Vagavona method of teaching pointe, with warm up on soft shoes first, is quite different that in the U.S. where girls typically buy their first pair of pointe shoes at a younger age. The Russian method requires waiting until students' muscles and tendons are strong enough to withstand the pressure of dancing on the tips of the toes, setting a solid foundation for an injury-free career.

Soon, the academy became the center of Olga's life as her love of ballet grew deeper and took root. Leaving school for summer vacation those first few years were difficult. She couldn't understand why she wasn't allowed to continue learning during the hot days of summer. "I cried when I had to leave for the summer. I was so focused on ballet and dedicated."

Olga thrived in the strict environment and diligently learned the basics despite comments by teachers during final exams that her shapely and muscular legs could prevent a future onstage career.

Her third year teacher, Irina Sirova, a former soloist with the Perm Opera Ballet, was also skeptical that Olga could have a career at the Bolshoi because she didn't have long, thin legs and a tall frame, the ideal model the Bolshoi Ballet seemed to favor. Olga was petite and thin, yet had already developed strong, muscular legs as a result of years of gymnastics to improve her spine.

Sirova actually discouraged Olga from a dancing career, saying it would be too difficult because her legs didn't look right for classical ballet. Despite her teacher's pessimism, Olga pressed on.

Many other instructors, including the tough minded Golovkina, praised Olga for her strong technique and graceful artistry. She carried herself differently than her classmates and she stood out for having that *it* quality.

A few times during the year, Olga and her classmates sat in on sessions where older advanced students practiced difficult combinations, movements the younger ones dreamed of learning. It was always a treat for Olga to watch the school's most famous male teacher, Pytor Pestov, instruct his dynamic students in the studio. And it was even more thrilling to watch two boys in particular, Vladimir Malakhov and Alexei Ratmansky, both of whom were two years ahead of Olga.

Although the entire school recognized that both of them, especially Malakhov, were star students, they were treated like everyone else. "We looked at them like, 'Oh, my gosh. They're so brilliant. [Malakhov] was a star because of his excellent body and enormous talent. He looks like a classical prince, with beautiful legs and a beautiful line." Malakhov, the youngest principal dancer to join the Moscow Classical Ballet, has danced with the world's leading ballet companies and is widely considered one of the best classical male dancers to come out of the Bolshoi academy in the last several decades.

Ratmansky is one of the most celebrated young choreographers in the world today. He danced with the Ukrainian National Ballet, the Royal Winnipeg Ballet, and the Royal Danish Ballet in a stellar career before taking over the Bolshoi Ballet Theater as its artistic director from 2004-08. He not only ushered in a new era in Russian ballet by bringing in fresh choreography from around the world but also elevated the Bolshoi's reputation even higher than that of the Kirov Ballet in St. Petersburg. As young dancers, these boys inspired many students including Olga.

In her fourth and fifth years, Olga's instructor, Tamara Yakovleva, showed more confidence in her young charge than the previous teacher. But by the middle of her fifth year, Olga, now fifteen, grew more worried more about her weight as did most of her classmates. The pressure to be thin was enormous and many girls in the school took drastic measures to keep their weight down including taking harmful diuretics.

The girls obsessed about their weight and many went on starvation diets consisting of little or nothing for breakfast, usually hot tea and some cheese, a lunch at the school cafeteria of red beet salad and more tea, without sugar, a small green salad for dinner and nothing to eat after 6 p.m. Sometimes after school on Saturdays, Olga would walk with friends to the subway and stop at a coffee shop for an indulgence of chocolate.

During one school day that winter, Golovkina came to observe Yakovleva's classical dance class which made the girls both excited at the prospect of catching the eye and favor of the school's hard-to-please director and extremely nervous too. Afterwards, Golovkina spoke with Yakovleva about several girls in the class and named Olga as one of the best.

The compliment sent Olga flying high, yet she still wrestled with her self-image. She could not overcome the peer pressure to become as skinny as possible. Regularly, the school checked students' weight and if a girl was too heavy, she could be asked to leave the program. For the weigh-ins, everyone went to the first floor medical offices where they stepped onto a scale and were weighed and measured with the numbers recorded in a journal.

The day before one particular weigh-in, Olga and a few classmates decided to take a drastic measure to ensure their weight would be their lowest possible. They went to a pharmacy near the school that dispensed strong diuretics on the black market to many Bolshoi Ballet Academy students. Olga and the girls bought the medicine and took it that evening.

The next morning during their ballet class they started having physical pain and discomfort.

"When class started, we felt sick and without energy. After the second combination, one girl asked the teacher, 'I don't feel good. May I sit down?' The teacher said, 'Yes, of course.' After a few combinations, another girl said, 'May I sit down?' I thought, 'I will not ask to sit, I can hold it.' In the middle of the barre, I felt really bad. The teacher came over to me and asked, 'Are you OK?' It was easy to see something was wrong with me. I said, 'Yes, I'm fine.' Finally, I just collapsed."

Olga ended up at the school doctor's office where she explained she was watching her weight and hadn't eaten anything. She was careful not to say what she had taken. She was afraid to admit she took a harmful drug. She was so obsessed with having her lowest weight recorded that day that while still being treated in the office Olga asked the nurse to weigh her and record it in the journal. They did, and then they called her father, who took her home where she spent the next several days recuperating. "It was a stupid thing to do," Olga said. "It's dangerous and it's not right. It doesn't work. It's only bad for your muscles. You can change your body the right way. It's very difficult to do, but you can get results after a few years. For ballet dancers, the problem is how you look onstage. Everybody knows that it's better if you have long, slim legs and arms."

Olga didn't have time to lose her momentum in the program. She had the annual final exam coming up in June that would literally determine the course of her life. Students' dancing ability and their looks were scrutinized; every detail was examined to ensure they had what it took for the final three years of preparation ahead. They would have to be ready at graduation by age eighteen to go directly into a professional ballet company, and for some that meant the Bolshoi Ballet.

Before the exam, Olga felt nervous but confident. She and the other students had practiced for months a difficult combination they would perform for Golovkina and the other instructors in one of the ballet studios. After everyone danced, their teacher went into Golovkina's office for a closed-door meeting that lasted for hours. The dancers changed out of their leotards and tights and into their regular clothes then sat in the hallway outside. When she finally emerged, Yakovleva read aloud each name and the grade they received.

Yakovleva had rehearsed this process with her girls each month to ensure improvement in their technique and so they could become more familiar with the competition system. During the monthly rehearsals, Olga received a score of *five*, which was the highest and the best. The teachers recognized Olga's enormous talent and knew she could become a ballerina, not just a ballet dancer. But at the end of year, no matter how flawless Olga performed, she wasn't able to receive a *five* because the judges always commented on her muscular legs. This time, at the conclusion of her fifth year, both Olga and her teacher were disappointed she received a *three* which came with judges' remarks on her muscular legs. Olga and Yakovleva were expecting a higher mark.

Olga worked hard to prepare a technically outstanding combination and receiving a *three* meant there was room for improvement. Despite the score, Olga knew she had the support of the instructors who saw her potential and considered her one of the academy's best.

With only three years from graduation, Olga joined an existing group of girls taught by the renowned teacher Ludmila Bogomolova-Nikonova, a former Bolshoi prima ballerina known for her powerful and energetic stage presence and brilliant technique. Nikonova became friends with her students, a normal part of Russian ballet culture which is considered helpful to enhance the creative process between teacher and student. She worked passionately to help her students bring out their own personality onstage.

"She was very tough and it was a lot of discipline but at the same time she treated us like professional dancers, not like students. It gave me confidence. She taught us to be patient with music and bring everything together; technique, pauses, lines, listening to the music and acting. The most important idea was to make our bodies, even our faces, and the movement come alive."

Olga trained under Nikonova for classical ballet. While students and teachers formed close bonds of friendship, teachers did at times have to resort to prodding, yelling, and cajoling to get their students to understand what they are learning and why. Placement and movement and using correct muscles is crucial; these instructors were known for pressing their fingers under students' derrieres to get them to squeeze and clench certain muscles properly. This exacting work can produce great artists and helps define the formidable Russian style.

Often teachers invited other instructors to watch their students during class. Natalia Zolotova, a well-respected teacher at the academy who also coached Nina Ananiashvili, saw Olga's class one day and commented to Nikonova afterwards. "You have one girl who will become a principal ballerina," Zolotova said, referring to Olga. Zolotova studied with Maria Romanova, the mother of Galina Ulanova, Russia's first *prima ballerina assoluta*, an extraordinary title shared in Russia only with Maya Plisetskaya, who would greatly influence Olga's later professional career.

Beyond the requisite technique courses, the academy stressed the importance of three key principles that, when followed, created an accomplished dancer who communicates depth onstage: the source of the creative process is deep within one's soul, dance is the means of that creative expression, and the body is the instrument. If students understood and eventually mastered the whole concept, they could become outstanding dancers.

Olga's acting teacher, Tatiana Pavlovitch, perhaps best illustrated how these elements came together. She taught method-style acting based on the form dramatist and writer Anton Chekov made famous, causing students to dig deep within. "For me, Tatiana was like a river or a lake on a very hot day. I was young but I felt I could get much more from her. She expressed the truth. Tatiana was a person who went real deep. She's been with me all of my professional life."

Olga also felt this way about her partnering coach Mark Ermolov, who reinforced the idea of making the audience feel what's in your heart. And from her character dance instructor, Viktor Borisov, Olga learned how the subtle nuances of character dance, within a classical framework, can create onstage magic.

Most of the students in Nikonova's class had trained with her for two years prior, so Olga was among a handful of newcomers to the class that the group considered fierce competition. Nikonova saw in Olga her potential to become a great ballerina and often during class paid attention to her promising student. Others in the class made their resentment known to Olga.

Each month, Nikonova graded her student's technical ability to prepare them for final exams which grew more competitive as graduation neared. Olga worried about how she would do in front of Golovkina and other instructors but took comfort in assurances from Nikonova. "She said, 'You're good, you're my best girl. If you're doing well, everything will be okay. Don't worry.' "

On the day of the exam, Olga and the other dancers in her group performed before Golovkina and the other teachers, then waited for hours for the results. When Nikonova emerged to report the results, she read aloud several names who received a *five* and several more who earned a *four.* Then they handed out the *threes* and Olga didn't hear her name. "I couldn't believe that I didn't get a *five* or a *four.* What did I get? If I got a *two* that meant I would have to leave the school."

Olga received a *two.* Devastated, she couldn't understand what happened. The only thing she thought was that she wasn't good enough and failed. It never occurred to her the low grade was a political move to get her out of the academy and had nothing to do with her ability. She couldn't possibly have known the real reason and it would be years later before she found out.

"I was sure it was because I was not good enough. I have so much drive and passion and love of ballet. Almost my whole life I've fought with myself. When you think you're not good enough, you continue to work and develop and keep going."

The academy instructors, who knew Olga was one of the best students, encouraged her parents to write a letter to the school asking permission to stay. Nikonova was surprised and saddened her brightest student was being forced out. In an effort to help Olga salvage her ballet training, she suggested Olga attend an open class with the Perm Ballet School and its famously stringent artistic director Ludmila Sakharova. If Olga was accepted into the Perm program, she could still graduate from a respected academy and fulfill her dream of becoming a ballerina. Perm school officials were visiting in Moscow and rehearsing at a nearby theater. The school is considered Russia's third best, behind the Bolshoi and Vaganova academies. So Olga went to the class and after doing a few basic combinations for Sakharova, she was asked to join the school.

But the young woman was heartbroken facing the possibility of going to Perm to dance. It was so far away from her home and parents in Moscow and, to her, it meant she failed at being at the country's top dance academy. Olga was distraught and didn't know what to do. Nikonova wanted Olga to succeed but knew she was powerless to change Golokvina's decision. So she hatched a plan.

Nikonova contacted her former husband, Stanislav Vlasov, and asked him to bring Olga into his small ballet company, the Moscow Chamber Ballet, for the summer to gain performance experience. Vlasov, a former principal with the Bolshoi Ballet, used to partner Sofia Golovkina and knew her well. He was, however, most famous for partnering with Ekaterina Maximova in an astounding performance of *Walpurgis Night* where he sent her soaring in the air with a one-handed lift.

Nikonova knew after Vlasov saw the teen dance he would see her enormous potential. If he wrote a letter to the school promising to hire Olga after graduation there was a good chance Golovkina would readmit her so she could graduate. It was Olga's best hope.

She had just turned sixteen and got her Soviet Union passport, which allowed her to travel outside of Moscow, but within the country, without her parents. All summer long, Olga rehearsed with the company, which then toured to the Ukrainian city, Kerch, and several other resort towns cupping the Black Sea.

Olga was in the corps de ballet when the troupe performed *Les Sylphides*, *Paquita Grand pas classique*, *Don Quixote Grand pas* and *Walpurgis Night*, Vlasov's signature role. Olga learned all of the corps de ballet parts of each ballet. One evening, as the cast was already in make-up and costumes, Olga was told she would dance with a group of six girls in the *Don Quixote Grand pas*. She didn't know the steps that well so some of the dancers quickly showed her backstage. "I was surprised, it happened so fast. It wasn't difficult technically, I learned to be fast and on time with everyone with the music."

By the end of the summer, Vlasov contacted Golovkina saying he intended to hire Olga as a professional and could she please finish her education.

Golovkina held a meeting with the school's instructors to decide Olga's fate and that of another student at the time. The headmistress presented the letters from Olga's parents and Vlasov then told the group Olga should not be allowed back. The teachers started arguing with her that Olga was unquestionably the best student in the academy and had to be readmitted. Golovkina got quiet then eventually relented. Seeing she was outnumbered, she allowed Olga back in the school.

Olga felt renewed returning to the academy in the fall of 1986 and wanted to succeed even more and prove she was worthy of a judge's *five*. She wondered all summer whether she would get to complete her education at the school that had become her second home. Confusion filled her head. She felt she wasn't as good as the rest of her classmates, yet was thrilled to have worked all summer with a professional company and found touring exciting especially to parts of the country unfamiliar to her. She was grateful to continue pursuing her dream of becoming a ballerina, but she was still bewildered why she scored so poorly on the previous year's final exam.

To her already jealous classmates, Olga's return signaled even more competition. She was the only one who worked all summer in a professional company, a deal arranged by their well-respected instructor. The onstage and touring experience proved priceless and put her even further ahead of her classmates. "There was probably a lot of competitive things going on, but at the time I didn't realize it. I was so focused on ballet."

A highlight of her student career was when her partnering teacher, Mark Ermolov, cast her in a school performance of *Strauss's Waltz* with a male student one year older. This meant Olga was technically advanced enough to keep up with a young man who was a grade ahead. She was honored that this teacher, whom she highly respected, recognized her talent.

Of course, Nikonova saw Olga's advancement too after her summer tour and she paid even more attention to her in class. Olga could hardly know how deep the resentment ran in at least one other classmate and how far someone would go to try to get her out of the school.

CHAPTER 5

AGAINST THE ODDS

ONE DAY, OLGA'S PARENTS RECEIVED a phone call from the Soviet government Office of the Minister of Culture. An official, on the other end of the phone, said they received a letter of complaint about the Bolshoi Ballet Academy's Artistic Director Sofia Golovkina and instructor Ludmila Nikonova. The letter was signed "from the parents of Olga Pavlova." Officials had opened an investigation over this, and the man on the phone asked what the couple knew about it. Completely shocked by this news, Valentina and Alexander Pavlov told the ministry official they never sent such a letter and made an appointment to sit down with the head of the education division in the Ministry of Culture to discuss it. They were shown the letter, which contained vicious accusations about Golovkina and Nikonova. It was made to look like it came from the Pavlovas, as the signature was typed and signed "the parents of Olga Pavlova" with both of their first names.

Alexander told them they didn't write the letter and the accusations were false. He also met privately with Golovkina and told her the same thing. He expressed worry about Olga, who was clearly being targeted by someone trying to get her expelled. Golovkina thanked him for coming in to explain the situation.

Who would send such a letter? Who wanted Olga out of the school in the worst way?

At the time, Olga knew of none of this. Her parents chose not to tell her about the letter until years later when she was well into her professional career. They knew it could be too much for their fragile daughter if she knew someone in her school went to such lengths to try to get her out. She would be devastated with worry and perhaps unable to continue dancing.

Even though Olga didn't know about it, the letter tremendously affected how she was treated in those last few years at school. She was overlooked and ignored by Golovkina and wasn't given significant roles in special academy performances held a few times each year at the Bolshoi Ballet and Kremlin theaters. The most favored students got top roles. Golovkina even thwarted a potential job offer for Olga near graduation with the prestigious Stanislavsky and Nemirovich-Danchenko Music Theater, Russia's third largest theater after the Bolshoi and St. Petersburg's Mariinsky. Olga assumed she was not as good as her classmates and drove herself to work even harder trying to be unattainably perfect.

Ironically, Olga and her parents never found out who sent the scathing letter, but it was a cowardly act of trying to get her out at any cost. (Dramatic rivalries and scandals are nothing new at the Bolshoi, both the ballet and its school. The most violent act came in the Jan. 17, 2013 attack of Bolshoi Artistic Director Sergei Filin, who was left partially blind after an assailant threw acid in his face. Disgruntled Bolshoi Dancer Pavel Dmitrichenko and his accomplices are serving prison time for the crime.)

At the end of her seventh year at the school, Olga received a mark of *four* from Golovkina in the final exam. With only one more year until graduation, Nikovona knew she had to help Olga stay on top and continue to outshine her classmates. That summer, she asked Olga to come to her home for private lessons. But the former Bolshoi ballerina walked a fine line. She wanted to help her best student, yet she didn't want to anger Golovkina because her youngest son, André Nikonov, was also a student at the school at the same level as Olga, and Nikonova didn't want to jeopardize his position there.

Nikonova privately instructed Olga to help make her technique more radiant. They worked from inside Nikonova's beautifully appointed Moscow apartment and at the school. The grueling preparation continued that next year when Nikonova cast Olga for a school performance of

La Fille Mal Gardée in the principal female role. When Golovkina found out about the casting decision, she squarely told Nikonova, "Why are you letting her dance the principal role? She will never become a principal ballerina."

During rehearsal in the studio, Nikonova had Olga run through her physically challenging variation three consecutive times without stopping. Olga danced the beautiful variation on pointe then finished and bowed, then she was instructed to run to the opposite corner of the studio and do it all over again. She wanted Olga to deliver a flawless performance and make it look easy onstage, and her drill sergeant-like method best accomplished that.

"You will have to do much better than anyone else," her teacher said. "You must do brilliantly because of your situation." She prepared Olga for the exam at nearly the same intensive level as an Olympic athlete. This was not the way Russian ballet dancers rehearse, Nikonova told her student, but this method would produce quicker results.

"She told me don't give up. On the day of the performance, it was easy for me. I wasn't even tired because I did it only once. Many other teachers said, 'Congratulations, you did real well. You caught the right character. That was exactly how it should be.'"

During her eighth and final year, Olga went to Golovkina, at the urging of her teacher, and asked for bigger parts in upcoming performances held at theaters outside of the academy. The school often showcased its students on Moscow's grand stages in shows where the country's top ballet stars turned out to watch the rising talent. Surprised that this rather shy student showed moxie and came to ask for a role, Golovkina gave Olga two principal parts; a complete *pas de deux* from *Laurencia*, a ballet made famous by Maya Plisetskaya with her amazing jumps, and the other, a solo in *Classical Symphony*, choreographed by Leonid Lavrovsky for the Bolshoi Ballet Academy with music by Sergey Prokofiev.

As for her own dancing, Golovkina was a former Bolshoi ballerina from the late 1930s until her appointment as the school's director in 1960. Plisetskaya, who danced with Golovkina at the Bolshoi during those early years and knew her well, bitingly describes the headmistress as a "talent-less, card-carrying Bolshevik Party member" in her 1992 autobiography, "*I Maya Plisetskaya.*"

"*She couldn't dance at all,*" *Plisetskaya wrote. "She would wobble doing pirouettes and chaînés but didn't fall over. It was like the Leaning Tower of Pisa. She possessed neither spirit nor brilliance. She used her lips to assist her as she danced, as if chewing gum. Her performances reeked of boredom and mediocrity. Audiences languished and applauded sparingly. In her younger days, she had gotten herself promoted to soloist by sharing a connubial bed with the venerable ballet master Fyodor Lopukhov, who had been the head of the Bolshoi Ballet for a short period before the [Second World] war. Their marriage was brief, but the spicy aspersiona Golovkina cast at Komsomol meetings left a certain mark on the history of the Moscow ballet . . .*"

As head of the Bolshoi academy, Golovkina's leadership was not questioned or besmirched publically. With Olga, she could be cunning and devastatingly strict. In one school performance, Olga was scheduled to partner with a younger student in the adagio *pas de deux* from *Don Quixote*. As with the classical *pas de deux* formula, there's *entrée*, *adagio*, male and female solos, and *coda*. After the *adagio*, Olga was to rest a few minutes while the male soloist went on, then Olga would return to the stage for her solo, the famous variation of the character Kitri holding the Spanish fan in her hand, before the *coda*. Golovkina, sitting in the audience, changed her mind midway through the show and cancelled the male solo portion leaving Olga no time to catch her breath before going right into her solo. It wasn't ideal, but Olga still nailed the performance.

The young ballerina continued pushing herself in class and during rehearsal for student performances. But during one in particular, for a challenging four-couple part in Leonid Yakobson's *Shuralé*, Olga felt like giving up. Her partnering coach, Mark Ermolov, taught her a lesson that has stuck with her ever since. He took a *pas de deux* and created a dance for four couples from *Shuralé*, a ground-breaking ballet from the 1950s crafted with Yakobson's unique vision around a Tatar folktale with elements of classical ballet, commedia dell'arte, and surrealism. Yakobson, who died in 1975, was a former ballet master at the Bolshoi and Kirov ballets and is widely considered as influential a choreographer as Balanchine and Mikhail Fokine.

When Ermolov explained a nuance of one of the choreographed movements that took Olga out of her comfort zone, she complained to him she couldn't do it. After an encouraging word from him, she continued but was still frustrated. Again, she said, "I can't." He looked at her and said, "If you can't, I'll get someone else to do it." He had Olga sit down while he called over another classmate who stepped in to learn the part. After class, Olga went to Ermolov to apologize, saying she was willing to tackle the part again. He said, "No, I won't change my decision. Learn from this that you should never say you can't." Olga was upset that she had allowed this small role to slip away from her but she learned never again to complain that she couldn't do something.

As graduation neared, Olga considered which company she wanted to dance with, as she knew a Bolshoi career would be impossible. It certainly helped that academy students regularly attended performances of Moscow's three top ballet companies, the Bolshoi, the Stanislavsky and Nemirovich-Danchenko Music Theater, and the Moscow Classical Ballet, and they took in their whole repertories over several seasons. Olga adored the Stanislavsky and Nemirovich-Danchenko Music Theater's repertoire including its memorable performance of *La Esmeralda*, which, at the time, was not in the repertory of the Bolshoi or Moscow Classical. *La Esmeralda*, a captivating, romantic three-act ballet full of passion, lust, and betrayal based on Victor Hugo's *"The Hunchback of Notre Dame"* is more familiar to American audiences as *Beauty and the Beast*. *La Esmeralda*, set to music by Cesare Pugni, is wildly popular with Russian audiences and follows the tale of Esmeralda, a gypsy girl, who is pursued by a wicked priest, betrayed by the man she loves and prized above all others by Quasimodo, the grotesque hunchback. While American audiences have seen mainly the famous *pas de deux Diana and Acteon* from this, which is unrelated to the original story, Russian companies have performed the entire ballet since the nineteenth century. Jules Perrot choreographed the work for his wife, ballerina Carlotta Grisi, in 1844. A generation later, Marius Petipa staged a 1886 production in St. Peterburg, Russia. But until recently, the 1935 version restaged by Agrippina Vaganova for the Kirov Ballet has been the foundation for most Russian productions.

La Esmeralda's blend of realism, romanticism, and dance acting spoke to Olga's heart. "It's a true dramatic performance like *La Bayadére* or *Giselle*. There was a lot of material for an actress to work with. The structure is perfect; the drama, story, choreography, music, stage sets, costumes and dancers. When it all comes together, it's magic."

After taking classes with Stanislavsky and Nemirovich-Danchenko Music Theater, its artistic director showed interest in Olga. Word came back to the young dancer this company wanted to hire her after graduation. She also took classes with the Moscow Classical Ballet that also expressed interested in giving her a contract. Olga's former classmate two years ahead, Vladimir Malakhov, a brilliant technician and artist whom she admired, was that company's youngest principal dancer.

During this time in the Bolshoi Ballet Academy's history, Golovkina decided which job offers graduates would take from the various ballet theaters. The dancers had no choice but to go along with Golovkina's wishes. The Bolshoi Ballet, naturally, got first choice of students they wanted to hire, then Stanislavsky and Nemirovich-Danchenko Music Theater and then Moscow Classical Ballet. After those offers were accepted, other theaters around the Soviet Union asked for Bolshoi graduates, and Golovkina had the power to send young dancers, who didn't have offers from the big three, to far-away places for jobs. Dancers were obligated to stay and work at a state-run company for three years before they could leave and go where they wished. But perestroika put an end to the mandatory three-year commitment in the early 1990s when dancers were free to leave a company anytime to pursue other avenues, and Golovkina lost her power to make job choices for the dancers. In 2001, she stepped down after forty-one years and was replaced in 2002 by Marina Leonova, a former Bolshoi dancer.

Olga's hopes were high until just a few days before graduation when she heard that Golovkina told the Stanislavsky and Nemirovich-Danchenko Music Theater that Olga would not join them. This theatrical company, with its *very* long name, was founded in 1898 by Konstantin Stanislavsky (1863-1938) and Vladimir Nemirovich-Danchenko (1858-1943). Stanislavsky created a method of training actors, which is still used today and focuses on the importance of the ensemble over the individual.

Golovkina's assistant, a former Bolshoi dancer who also served as a partnering teacher for boys at the school, called Olga into his office one day for a strange sort of meeting.

"He said, 'Be prepared, if anyone comes in and sees you here, I'll have to start yelling at you. I'm just acting, but go along with it. I'm not supposed to be talking with you.'" Then he shared that Golovkina and the Stanislavsky artistic director got into a heated argument after the headmistress forbid Olga from joining the company. They had one opening for a female dancer and they wanted Olga. But Golovkina refused it, and the position went to another student. Once again, Olga was devastated she was so close to graduating and had no job prospect.

Little did she know that prospects were growing brighter for her. Friends in her graduating class, Alexei Kremnev, her boyfriend at the time, and two others were auditioning for Moscow's Children's Musical Theatre, now called the Natalia Satz Theatre, which performs music, dance, and opera. On a whim, Olga decided to join her classmates at an audition but had no intension of trying out. The afternoon ended with the theater's dance choreographer offering all of them jobs after graduation. (Presently Kremnev is the artistic director of the school of the Joffrey Ballet in Chicago.) Although Olga politely said she would consider the job, the perfectionist inside her felt like she had somehow failed. She bought into the perception held by her peers and teachers that the best ballerinas become part of the Bolshoi brand, and dancers who go elsewhere, especially to a smaller theater, aren't as good. It would be later in her career that she realized this wasn't true and, more importantly, finding the right mentors to help her develop her art often meant going off the prescribed path.

Still, Olga wanted to dance for one of the top three companies and this theater, although well respected in Moscow, didn't quite match the standard she had set for herself. She was still holding out for Moscow's no. three ballet company, Moscow Classical.

The Children's Musical Theatre is one of the city's crowning jewels in the performing arts as little expense was spared to build the facility that could easily accommodate a symphony orchestra as well as sizeable sets for both opera and ballet. Its repertoire, at the time, included *Madame Butterfly*, *Cinderella*, and *Peter and the Wolf.*

Although the theater and Satz are widely known throughout Russia, little is known of her in the West. Satz directed the theater in 1935 when the celebrated Russian composer Sergei Prokofiev and his wife brought their two young sons there to see an opera, *The Tale of the Fisherman and the Goldfish*. Satz, thrilled that the famous family returned and became regular patrons, started thinking how she could have Prokofiev create something for her theater. She came up with the idea to craft a musical piece that would teach children about the sound and character of orchestral instruments. At her invitation, Prokofiev wrote *Peter and the Wolf* using a narrative to help listeners distinguish the different orchestral sounds, with each character relating to its own instrument; the bird, a chirping flute, the duck, a resounding oboe, the cat, a dulcet clarinet, Peter's imposing grandfather, the bassoon, and the frightening wolf, three horns. Later that year, the theater staged a test run of *Peter* with Prokofiev playing the music on the piano, while Satz narrated, entertainingly changing her voice to become each of the characters. The audience was a tiny group of children, about a dozen in all. Instantly it was a hit. Later, *Peter and the Wolf* premiered to a much larger audience and, of course, went on to become one of the composer's most recognizable works.

Just a few days before Olga's graduation, Stanislav Vlasov made good on his promise from two years earlier. When he brought Olga into his small Moscow Chamber Ballet for a summer, he told Golovkina he intended to hire her after graduation. Now with a formal written offer of employment sent to the school, Olga had to decide her future. She was living with an ongoing and looming dread. She didn't want to make a bad choice. If she turned down this offer and graduated without anything, she could be sent far away from her beloved Moscow to a remote part of the country to a company she didn't want to work for. She had to make a decision.

Her understanding teacher and friend Nikonova said she would talk with Moscow Classical to see if they would make an offer. Moscow Classical was mainly a touring company with an impeccable international reputation, managing to travel the world to perform even under the old, closed Soviet system. The prospect of world travel was very enticing to many young dancers.

But the company was busy preparing to leave for a United Kingdom tour just a day after Olga's graduation. The company director said after the tour, they could make an offer. For Olga, this meant graduating with nothing but a promise and no signed offer. She just couldn't take that risk, not after all that Golovkina had put her through.

Students knew final exams were critical in deciding which ballet company they would join. They were tested during a four-day exam period on ballet technique, partnering, character dance, and acting on stage. They also took a written state exam. During the ballet technique portion, students went through all the basics at the barre and at center then performed combinations set to music and finished with jumps. Then the girls put on tutus and pointe shoes and showed what they learned en pointe, including 32 fouetté turns from *Swan Lake*.

In the audience was Nikolai Simachev, Bolshoi's ballet master who had a long and successful career as a principal dancer with the company and was best known for his character acting. All of the judges, except Golovkina, wanted to give Olga a *five*, which would automatically earn her the *"red"* diploma, a crowning achievement that gives a dancer direct admission into a choreographic institute.

Golovkina forbid Olga to be granted a *five*.

Even though Simachev told Golovkina that Olga was the best-trained girl among the entire graduating class (eighteen were hired by the Bolshoi Ballet that year) and Olga received *five's* in all but one category, Olga took home a *four*. She was at her lowest weight ever, but Golovkina kept her from a perfect score because of her shapely legs and presumably more.

Soon afterward, Golovkina called Olga into a meeting with several people who helped her throughout her academy years; Ludmila Nikonova, Stanislav Vlasov, and people from the Children's Theatre. Olga was nervous and felt her heart pounding fast. Remembering Vlasov's promise to hire her, she sat at the conference table, looking down, avoiding eye contact with everyone. Golovkina announced to the group that Olga had two offers, one from the Moscow Chamber Ballet, the other from the Children's Theater. Which one did she want? In her heart, she wanted Moscow Classical, but that wasn't going to happen. Olga could not lift her eyes to look at Vlasov, not after all he had done on her behalf. She could never repay him and now, she was going to reject his offer. How could she ever face him? And Ludmila too, went such lengths to help. They would both think Olga was terrible for making her decision, she thought. A sick feeling rolled around inside her stomach, yet she knew she had no other option. Olga agreed to accept the offer from Moscow's Children's Musical Theatre.

CHAPTER 6
THE MAKING OF
A BALLERINA

She began her professional career in the corps de ballet in Moscow's Children's Musical Theatre in August 1988. This wasn't the place she had imagined starting out. Still disappointed she was kept from the Stanislavsky and Nemirovich-Danchenko Music Theater, Olga was depressed. On the outside, she seemed eager to start with the company but inside she felt discouraged. This was a children's theater, after all, and the roles she imagined getting were that of a rabbit or a cat instead of more meatier parts in classical ballets for adults.

She could hardly know that she was actually in the right place and that this theater would allow her to start to become the ballerina of her dreams. She would have to credit the influence of one woman, Eleonora Vlasova, a coach at the Children's Theatre. Though Olga started in the corps, she didn't stay there for long. As rehearsals began for *Cinderella*, the artistic director immediately saw the recent graduate's potential, and Olga was given the principal role, as well as several solo parts. She was paired with Dmitri Roudnev in the starring role. This meant Olga started working with Vlasova, a famous and beautiful prima ballerina who had danced with many great partners including Rudolph Nureyev prior to his defection to the West. Olga, while at her lowest point emotionally, recalls meeting Vlasova.

"She was a really strong woman. She took me and kind of shook me and said, 'You have to work. This is not the end of your life.'"

The excitement of working with Vlasova helped breathe new life into Olga. The chance to work with one of the country's beloved ballerinas came about only by accepting the lesser job offer. Her new mentor wasted no time in starting to shape Olga's burgeoning career and help bring the true ballerina out of the young dancer. "She did amazing things for me. I was very lucky to meet her, it was a miracle. She was such a great teacher, it was a big thing for me. When I graduated and started work, I was a little bit depressed. She pulled me out from this condition and she pushed me to work. And she definitely got me to the next level."

Lesson number one: Hard work is the ticket to success. She pushed Olga during long hours of practice. Jokingly, Olga said Vlasova didn't allow her to leave the ballet studio. She taught Olga how to watch, learn, and think about each movement and to discover why each movement is performed a certain way. In essence, she learned to dig deeper into her own soul.

During one rehearsal in particular, Vlasova saw that Olga was doing *pas de chat*, quick catlike steps that spring from one foot to the other, with a small nuance in the coordination that was not correct. Vlasova told Olga she had made a mistake but didn't point out what it was. She wanted Olga to find it on her own. Vlasova demonstrated the right way to do it, then challenged Olga to find the difference between the two.

"She pushed me to find this mistake myself. It's very hard work because it requires lots of patience. We worked on this for probably two hours, and I could not tell where my mistake was. It was such a little thing, it would have been easier for her just to explain it to me. But her goal was to teach me to find the mistake myself."

When Olga figured it out, she realized her teacher had helped her grow.

"She pushed me to think as a teacher, she taught me how to look at myself in the mirror to find the best things and the worst things about myself. She told me, 'You have to develop your best things and show those to the audience while

continuing to work on your bad things. When you perform, make your bad things invisible. You will need this throughout your career.'"

Even the best ballerinas have their weaknesses. Not everyone has strong turns in both directions and some have trouble spinning. For Olga, her jumps, at the time, needed some work. With an upcoming performance just days away and little time to practice, Olga had to perfect a movement that was giving her trouble. Vlasova told her, "I'll work with you differently on this, I'll show you exactly each movement, technically and emotionally, and you'll repeat it. But I want to let you know, this is not a correct way to learn. We'll never work this way again.' We started to work and she pushed me to think about the movement and go real deep into the emotional drama."

As the two worked closely, Vlasova noticed that Olga would sit with her eyes down, not wanting to draw much attention to herself.

Lesson number two: Think like a prima ballerina. Olga learned how to present herself off stage as a confident, well-dressed women. "She told me, 'You have to feel like a ballerina, live like you're a diva,'" Olga said with a giggle. That meant looking like a proper ballerina off stage from head to toe; coiffed hair, nice make up, long fingernails, dressy clothing (denim jeans were *verboten*), heels, and a hat. Her student took the advice to heart and went out and bought an elegant red hat that looked like it belonged to the late Princess Diana of Wales. Olga wore it everywhere.

"'If you want to be a ballerina, you have to do this,'" Vlasova told her in no uncertain terms. " 'You cannot shrink.' She guided me as a person, as a ballerina, and as an actress."

By the end of her first season with the company in 1989, Olga made her professional debut as the star of *Cinderella*. This was truly the first time she danced like a ballerina. Though not even twenty years old, she met and married dancer Alexei Moskalenko, who also worked for the company.

The following season the troupe would perform in Germany, just months after the fall of the Berlin Wall and the beginning of perestroika. Satz, who at this time still presided over her theater, adored ballet and traveled with the company when they toured. This was the first time Olga was permitted by the government to leave Russia. Her first trip outside her country was to Prague in the fall of 1990. She and others from her ballet company traveled on a luxury tour bus. She had never seen such a nicely appointed vehicle before. As they crossed into Germany, she remembers looking out the window studying everything. The vista of quaint villages with neatly-landscaped cottage homes seemed charming with the fresh blanket of snow that had fallen; flowers of all different sizes still managed to peek through the white billowy powder.

The contrast between her life in Moscow and how people lived in Germany was stark for her and even more so for her maternal grandfather, Ivan Lomakin. When Olga returned home, Ivan asked her how the Germans lived in the West. He had served in the red army as a solider during World War II stationed in Vienna and was shot by a German solider during Stalin's march into the city. He recovered from bullet wounds in his ankle and hip at a military hospital before being sent back home to Russia to resume fighting.

"My grandfather asked me, 'How do they live in Germany?' I told him, 'Very nice. It's beautiful. I saw only one side though. I didn't have any problems and our hotels were very nice.' He told me, 'That's interesting. After the war, we won, but right now our life is so difficult. We put them down and now the German people have the opportunity to live a wonderful life.'"

While Ivan continued fighting in the war in 1941, the Soviet government moved his young wife, Zoya Lobanova, and other citizens out of Moscow and into small, rural villages that sorely lacked the infrastructure to provide any measure of a comfortable existence. The couple's tiny house had no heat or running water and an outhouse served as the bathroom. Bathing or washing dishes meant carrying water from a nearby well to the home. One small heater was used to survive the long frigid winter months. The villagers were isolated and there was no telephone service. The closest public phone was a twenty-minute walk to a train station. When her grandmother went shopping, buying food was difficult as shops were routinely out of basic staples and supplies. Going without eating was common. It was a harsh existence with no relief.

Olga knew her grandparents endured many hardships and she remained grateful she could have a better life, especially the ability to pursue her dream of becoming a ballerina.

After her second year with the Children's Musical Theater, Olga was growing restless and she knew it was time to move on.

The collapse of the Soviet regime changed everything throughout Russia. Some things opened quickly and the landscape started changing in the ballet world. For the first time, new freedoms allowed individuals to open smaller, private ballet companies. One of Moscow's famous ballet masters, the former Bolshoi teacher Alexander Prokofiev, organized his own company and hired many great dancers away from more established ones. "Everyone respected Prokofiev very much and I did too." Olga worked for Prokofiev's company briefly in 1990. That year, she also saw the break up of her very brief marriage to Moskalenko, a subject she prefers to not to talk about except to say the decision was mutual. Russian culture does not encourage an outward display of deep emotion. Many Russians keep their personal feelings to themselves.

Opportunity knocked again when Yuri Grigorovich, the famous longtime Bolshoi Ballet artistic director, hired Olga for his new company, the Bolshoi Ballet Grigorovich Company. Grigorovich ran both companies simultaneously. His new professional troupe performed some of the same repertoire as the Bolshoi Ballet and was also based inside the Bolshoi Theater and shared the same coaches. But the new company traveled outside of Russia far more than the Bolshoi. Olga, now a soloist with Grigorovich's company, journeyed around the world and went to Japan, North America, Europe, the Middle East and throughout Russia. The company kicked off the American leg of its tour in College Station, Texas before traveling to many large cities. College Station was the first U.S. city Olga visited, and the first time she had the chance to use the little English she had learned. After her academy graduation, she enrolled in English classes, but hardly used what she acquired until she started speaking conversationally while touring countries outside her homeland.

For the first time, Olga experienced the hectic pace of a dance troupe's international touring schedule which includes long flights, often with delays, nighttime shuttles to hotels, and early morning rehearsal at studios before performances. After shows, dancers quickly pack and board buses for the airport and head to the next destination. Seldom do they get one or two days respite between shows to sight see or catch up on sleep.

In between her grueling dance schedule, though, she found time to fall in love again. And she didn't have to look far. She met fellow dancer Ilya Kuznetsov during rehearsals and the pair later married.

"It was a great life. I was able to perform on the Bolshoi stage when we danced in Moscow. When we rehearsed, we spent so much time in the Bolshoi Theater, we were part of it. Every day you could meet Bolshoi stars and see their performances. Sometimes, the stars performed with us as guest artists. Rehearsing with Grigorovich was very interesting. To be close to a very talented, creative person is a great experience, and he was a genius."

Olga grew professionally and personally during this time. Although she began with the company in the corps de ballet, she soon rose to soloist roles and eventually principal ones in much of the classical repertoire including *The Nutcracker, Sleeping Beauty, Swan Lake, Raymonda* and *The Golden Age.*

Outside the theater, where these lavish productions took place, political discontent was brewing. Olga found herself caught in the Russian Constitution Crisis with its bloody crescendo on Oct. 3, 1993. The Bolshoi Theatre is located downtown near the Kremlin, which was cordoned off by military tanks and armed soldiers during this event. "When I took a cab into the downtown, the military stopped us each time and I had to show identification and proof that I was going to work." As the situation improved, military restrictions were lifted.

Despite the political climate, Olga found herself working again with two former Bolshoi Ballet Academy instructors, Tatiana Pavlovitch and Mark Ermolov, who helped prepare her for exciting career opportunities that lie ahead.

In 1995, the Grigorovich closed his company's doors and, at the same time, he was ousted as the Bolshoi's director of several decades. During the company's final tour of the U.S., many dancers decided to stay in America.

But Olga chose to return to Moscow and didn't even consider staying in the West at his point in her career.

"I thought I should be back in Moscow and continue to develop myself as a ballerina. With Grigorovich's company, I was a soloist, and I wanted to become a prima ballerina. I was really dedicated to classical ballet. I did what I wanted, and I performed all the classical repertoire. I didn't want to do anything else at the time and the best place to do this was Russia."

Olga, now twenty-five, found herself dancing not just for one company but three of Moscow's major companies; Moscow Classical Ballet, Renaissance Ballet Company and Imperial Russian Ballet, which was under the direction of Maya Plisetskaya, Russia's *Prima Ballerina Assoluta*. Olga kept a dizzying schedule and loved every minute of the crazy pace.

Getting to work with Plisetskaya at the Imperial Russian Ballet was the opportunity of a lifetime. The excitement of being around Russian ballet's *grande dame* was only part of the adrenaline rush Olga felt going between rehearsals and performances with these companies. Olga first met Plisetskaya while dancing with Grigorovich's company, and she often watched Plisetskaya at the Bolshoi Theater. "She was a real life diva. I saw her all the time but I never spoke with her."

With perestroika, the climate in Russia changed dramatically and shattered the accepted model of dancers working for one company their entire professional life. New freedom meant artists could now work for more than one company and they could freely travel outside the country as old government restrictions virtually vanished.

While Olga enjoyed the demanding work as a soloist for Moscow Classical and as a guest artist for the other companies, there would come a time when something had to give. Olga adored the Renaissance Ballet because of its high caliber coaches, who included former Bolshoi stars Raisa Struchkova and Nikolai Fadeyechev, a former partner and close friend of

Plisetskaya. There she also met the incomparable Nina Osipyan, a former principal ballerina with Moscow Classical, who would literally help change Olga's life and future. At the same time, Olga enjoyed performing the standard works of classical ballet for Moscow Classical, and starring as a guest artist for the Imperial Russian Ballet allowed her parts in formal galas where she performed *pas de deuxs* with new partners, often stars from other companies. All of this experience expanded her repertoire and exposed her to new choreography, which allowed her to grow and develop further as an artist. She was starting to develop more emotional depth in her dancing. Partnering with other great dancers and traveling to new places stretched her as a dancer. Marriage also enhanced her reservoir of expression. Slowly she was becoming the ballerina she always imagined.

At the Renaissance Ballet, Olga met Osipyan and loved her coaching methods. Eventually, both women left that company and joined the Imperial Russian Ballet, which was started in 1994 by former Bolshoi dancers Gedeminas Taranda and Nikolai Anokhine at the suggestion of Plisetskaya, who presided over the company.

Olga continued to learn the art of ballet with every new experience. But she would have no idea how pivotal the year ahead would be for her. Decisions made during this time in her life would have long lasting repercussions.

Alexander Pavlov, Valentina Pavlova and Olga, age five, at
the Black Sea in Russia. Photo credit: Olga Pavlova

Olga (second to last row on the left) with students in her Bolshoi
Ballet Academy class. Photo credit: Olga Pavlova

Olga and her coach Nina Osypian in Madrid, Spain. Photo credit: Olga Pavlova

(L to R) Ilya Kuznetsov, Maya Plisetskaya, Gedeminas Taranda, and Olga in 1996. Photo credit: Olga Pavlova

Olga performing the lead in *Giselle*, 2002. Photo credit: Olga Pavlova

As Odette/Odile in *Swan Lake* with the Kiev Opera
Ballet, 2001. Photo credit: Olga Pavlova

As Kitri in Don Quixote. Photo credit: Olga Pavlova

Olga in *La Bayadére*. Photo credit: Marty Sohl

Olga and Genya in Paul Mejia's *Webern Pieces*, 2009. Photo credit: Marty Sohl

Olga Pavlova and Genya Anfinogenov. Photo credit: Shelley Dalebout

CHAPTER 7

STARTING OVER

Now that Osipyan was coaching Olga, she could focus on a larger goal in mind. Osipyan had great success coaching other dancers at international competitions and she wanted the same for Olga. If this Bolshoi Academy graduate was to become a prima ballerina, she would need something special on her résumé to set her apart from others. Winning a gold medal at a worldwide contest could do just that.

But before the arduous competition training could begin, Osipyan had a far more daunting challenge for her student. For Olga to become a prima ballerina, she would need the ability to dance any repertoire. And to do that, she needed to start over *literally* in her training.

Though it sounded unthinkable for a professional at this level, Osipyan realized Olga's basic technique needed refining so she could master even the most difficult choreography anywhere. Although she was shocked by her coach's assessment, Olga knew in her heart her mentor was right.

"I realized that I needed it. I was so focused on rehearsing a lot, I just repeated the same things. I wasn't progressing well enough. I came to her and said, 'I'm ready to do everything you tell me.' I was twenty-five and my body already learned a lot, and I already performed as a soloist and sometimes in principal roles. Some dancers end their career at this age. Nina cautioned me that for the first few months, my body would repeat what it already knew and wouldn't learn anything new. 'You'll feel like you cannot do anything, like a beginning student,' she told me. 'That's a normal part of the process to teach your body to work differently.'"

Osipyan recalls this time with fondness. *"With Olga, we started at the beginning. It was great to work with her because she's so easy to be with and she wanted to learn. It was very interesting to see how my method could change the body. What I was able to teach her allowed her to continue dancing for a long time without any major injuries. I told her it will be hard work, and the first few months will be terrible. But work hard everyday and slowly you'll see the results."*

Osipyan used an intensive, hands-on approach that, at times, perhaps took on the quality of a sculptor shaping clay into a fine figure. Olga worked at the barre every day for hours. Slowly, she relearned basic technique, such as etching the floor with each pointed foot in *battement tendu* for twenty minutes while her coach sat on the floor watching and making adjustments to her legs and feet. This kind of personal training was extremely repetitious and mentally trying. "Sometimes I felt like I would go crazy because it was so tedious, like you're ready to kill yourself. Over and over I would tell myself I need this and to trust her."

During this one-on-one training, the two formed a special tight-knit bond, which has lasted for years. Osipyan knew exactly how it felt starting over in training. She was twenty-nine when she relearned from the great Russian ballerina Marina Semyonova, who became a teacher-répétiteur following a brilliant career that spanned the early-to-mid twentieth century. Semyonova, who died in 2010 just three days shy of turning 102, was a student of Agrippina Vaganova, the legendary teacher whose style, now adopted worldwide, is considered ballet's gold standard.

"When I came to Marina I started from the beginning," Osipyan said. *"Everything I did she said, 'No, wrong.' She could be quite abusive in class. We had Nadezhda Pavlova and others who were stars in class. For a very long time, I couldn't understand what I was doing wrong with technique. After about three years, I realized what Semyonova was doing and how she was teaching me this way. I was very fortunate that I met her and could pass that knowledge onto my students."*

Ballet is an art passed down hand to hand and Olga was a direct descendant of Vaganova.

After a few months, Olga started noticing the difference in her body and in her dancing. Her leg muscles were more elongated and she felt different onstage, more comfortable, more in control with every movement. Within a year, the difference was startling. "I felt like I was able to do anything, you feel like your body is an instrument that you can work with. It gave me a new freedom onstage I hadn't had before."

During this time of experiencing professional growth and a newfound freedom onstage, it was also a difficult period, laced with personal struggle. An impossibly busy schedule left Olga with little time to cultivate her marriage to Kuznetsov and cracks started to appear.

In between her intense studio retraining, she toured with Imperial Russian Ballet to many countries including Austria, Brazil, France, Finland, Germany, Japan, Portugal, Spain, and Uruguay from 1995 to 1996. In this time, she danced the company's mostly classical repertoire with other world-class artists. Being away from her husband for long stretches did little to help strengthen their union.

Plisetskaya often traveled with the touring troupe and sometimes oversaw rehearsals. Her approach to coaching dancers was amicable, especially when she made corrections and suggestions such as trying a movement differently from what they had rehearsed. "It was a very friendly atmosphere," Olga said. "We were all artists doing one artistic endeavor together."

Olga had the fortunate experience to learn one of ballet's best-known works, Alberto Alonso's *Carmen Suite* (1967), from the woman he created it for. *Carmen* became a signature role for Plisetskaya, and when it debuted in Russia it was also performed by Alicia Alonso, Alberto's sister-in-law, at Ballet Nacional de Cuba. The famous work is set to music by Rodion Shchedrin, Plisetskaya's husband. Although this production of *Carmen* was a shorter abridged version for gala performances, guest ballerinas were used to dance the lead. Olga studied Plisetskaya's coaching in every move and detail onstage and had hoped that one day she would get to dance the whole ballet.

By 1996, Olga was ready to enter an international professional ballet competition, and Osipyan suggested she enter the Rudolf Nureyev

International Ballet Competition held in Budapest, Hungary. Olga prepared with her partner and husband, Kuznetsov, to dance three *pas de deuxs* for the three-round competition from *La Sylphide*, *The Nutcracker* and *Le Corsaire*. After months of preparation, Olga, Kuznetsov, and Osipyan were off to Budapest. When they arrived, Olga was naturally quite nervous. After seeing so many other impeccably trained and experienced dancers from around the globe, she had difficulty concentrating on her variations and all the little things she needed to remember while performing. It didn't help that onstage warm up meant all of the competitors and their coaches shared the same floor at the same time.

Behind the scenes, the politics of the competitive ballet world were ever-present and even before the competition ended, final decisions had been rendered. One judge was U.S. ballerina Eva Evdokimova, who toured the world partnering Nureyev later in his career. Word around the competition surfaced that Evdokimova would refuse to judge favorably any Russian dancer purely out of vengeance. Years earlier, Evdokimova, the gold medal winner of the 1970 Varna International Competition, felt publicly embarrassed when she didn't place at a Moscow competition. Even the audience knew she deserved a higher prize than the diploma, the lowest accolade possible, she was awarded, and they booed a Soviet official at the awards ceremony.

Evdokimova was reported to have said, according to Osipyan, that when she served on a judge panel she would never let a Russian win. For this Budapest competition, she served on a panel with two other judges from St. Petersburg, Russia. Osipyan was stunned to learn that after just the first round of dancing, it was decided that a Hungarian dancer would receive the top honor. "Olga danced *La Sylphide* beautifully," Osipyan remembered. "But there was nothing we could do. I was so surprised that they awarded second and third place to very weak dancers, and a Hungarian girl took first."

The experience didn't dishearten Olga from wanting to try again at another competition, and she was now motivated to capture a gold medal.

But this time, her friends and some colleagues tried dissuading her from going through another lengthy preparation period and nerve-shattering competition. Ballet competition at this level is often more about bravura and impressing judges and less about the subtle artistry, emotional depth, and superb technique requisite to achieve greatness onstage. After all, her friends said she wasn't a competition girl, but that she shined her brightest in theatrically demanding roles that showed her masterful technique and expressive qualities.

To her credit, Olga didn't listen to them. Soon she found herself preparing again with Osipyan in the studio for the Maya (Plisetskaya) International Ballet Competition held in December 1996 in St. Petersburg on somewhat more familiar soil than Hungary. This time around, she would know what to expect and how to better mentally prepare.

She would partner with Kuznetsov for two of the four competitive dances.

By now, the couple's marriage of just a few years had crumbled. The stress of being apart for long periods of time, and the temptation that comes with it, proved too much. The pair divorced earlier in the year, though they maintained a working relationship.

Olga experienced a period of tremendous artistic growth during this time and her expressive range deepened even further. While her life seemed chaotic with a packed touring schedule, extra studio time preparing for the competition, and dealing with the emotional stress of a second divorce, the stage was her refuge as it had always been. When she slowed down long enough to rest on days off, she fought away sadness and loneliness that could easily creep in. She *lived* for rehearsal and performing on the road and focused on the thrill and creative stimulation of working with the company's troupe and its many acclaimed guest artists. This was an exciting time for her. She found herself partnering with major stars such as American Ballet Theater's Vladimir Malahov in *Les Sylphides*, the Bolshoi's Nikolai Tsiskaridze in *Sleeping Beauty*, and Alexei Ratmansky, who went on to become a world-renowned choreographer, in *Giselle*.

Her most intriguing role during this time was *Tango* with music by Astor Piazzolla. She partnered with Gedeminas Taranda, Imperial Russian Ballet's artistic director. Together, they delivered a flawless and emotionally charged performance, with Taranda's virtuosic qualities and Olga's delicate yet authoritative attack. Traditional *Argentine Tango* dancing calls for exquisite precision, deep expression, and sensual restraint and theirs was one of powerful contrasts, Osipyan remembers. "It starts out with the man looking around rather aloofly smoking a cigarette, then he casts it aside when he sees the woman. Olga's character is a lonely, vulnerable woman who needs support in life. They meet and passion strikes, real passion. Technically, they were brilliant and the tempo was lightning fast. In the end, he just sort of throws her away, casts her off like he used her and she's alone onstage."

Osipyan instinctively knew this *Tango* had enough spice, expression, and technical brilliance to leave a lasting impression on the Maya competition judges. In December, Olga and her partners and Osipyan arrived in St. Petersburg ready to compete on that frigid morning.

Olga danced with Kuznetsov in *Flower Festival in Genzano pas de deux* and *The Last Day of Judas* (choreographed by N. Androsov with music by Rodion Shchedrin), with Taranda the *Tango* and a short solo variation from *Don Quixote*.

"I vividly remember their *The Last Day of Judas*," Plisetskaya said, speaking in Russian from her home in Spain. As head of the competition, she recalled the impact of the couple's performance. "Olga was expressive, moving, so in touch with the music. I wish there were more performances like that." She also called Olga and Taranda's *Tango* "a masterpiece in miniature."

Hours after the competition ended, the judges announced that Olga had won first place. She came here to win and she did, now there could be no stopping her.

At the awards ceremony the following day, Olga was presented with a large, gold first place medallion from Plisetskaya, and a contract offer from Northern Ballet. During the gala that followed, Olga danced encore performances of *Flower Festival in Genzano* and *Tango*. That night was magical for Olga. She was in love with Taranda and wanted to be with him despite his reputation and the whispers she would hear from others in the ballet world about his fidelity to her.

She not only accomplished her goal of winning gold, but also noticed that people around her started treating her differently, more like a prima ballerina. It seems that starting over again in her training proved life changing and award winning. But Olga viewed the experience of winning gold with a practical eye. She was honored to win and it helped bolster her résumé giving her a newfound credibility within her circle.

But what about this offer from Northern Ballet? If she were to accept, it could take her career and life in a whole new direction. Inevitably she would become far better known in the West and seen by worldwide audiences, not just Russian. The opportunity for travel and new experiences seemed limitless.

Ultimately, she had to decide whether to stay in Moscow with Taranda and her family or take a giant leap into the unknown at Northern Ballet. Her decision wouldn't just be about dancing, it was about trading the comforts of her homeland and the man she was in love with for something new. What would she do?

CHAPTER 8

Prima Ballerina Assoluta

Maya Plisetskaya stands alone as the greatest Russian ballerina of the mid-twentieth century. During her forty-seven year career with the Bolshoi Ballet, her impeccable technique, theatrical stage presence, and beauty were unmatched by anyone. She is the gold standard in classical Russian ballet, though many speak of her alongside Anna Pavlova, who danced a generation before, and Galina Ulanova whom Plisetskaya replaced as the Bolshoi star when Ulanova retired. Olga is often asked if she's related to the great Anna Pavlova and while she isn't, she loves the connection people make with ballet's Pavlova before her.

From her earliest days, Plisetskaya stood out onstage. Her red hair, her cascading, fluid arms and pliable back that would softly bend like no one else's earned her superstar status. She was born to Jewish parents in 1925, joined the Bolshoi in 1943, and lived an incredible life of such stark contrasts that her story reads like fiction to Westerners unfamiliar with the harsh and formidable Soviet empire. Her father was killed during the Stalinist purges and her mother spent years in a *gulag*, a Soviet forced-labor camp, while Plisetskaya was raised in poverty by relatives. Her maternal aunt and uncle, Sulamith and Asaf Messerer, who are siblings, were Bolshoi dancers. They helped raise her and her brother Azari Plisetsky, the acclaimed Bolshoi dancer. Her aunt and uncle helped nourish Plisetskaya's passion for ballet despite living through the most squalid wartime and post-war conditions.

Shadowed and harassed by the KGB all of her professional life and prevented from leaving the country until 1959 at age thirty-four, Plisetskaya kept company with some of the world's most famous artists and cultural icons of her time including Coco Chanel, Salvador Dali, and the Hollywood elite, whom she wrote candidly about in her autobiography. Famed French designer Pierre Cardin dressed her both onstage and off. Marc Chagall painted her in grand murals that hung at Lincoln Center. She was so well known around the world that by the time Soviet officials allowed her to travel to Paris for the first time in 1961, after being a Bolshoi star for many years, she was received at the legendary Maxim's by many of its famous clientele.

Although known for her signature role in the *Dying Swan*, a part first danced by Anna Pavlova, Plisetskaya is inseparably connected to *Anna Karenina*, a tragic portrayal of Leo Tolstoy's novel that immortalized her beauty and theatrical prowess. American audiences saw *Anna Karenina* for the first time when the Bolshoi toured the U.S. in the early 1960s. When she met First Lady Jacqueline Kennedy in 1962 at the White House, Mrs. Kennedy greeted her with a smile and a warm handshake and reportedly exclaimed, *"You really are Anna Karenina!"*

The year after she was permitted to travel outside the Soviet Union, Nikita Khrushchev presented Plisetskaya with the highest ballet honor, *prima ballerina assoluta*, an Italian title which literally means absolutely the very best ballerina. It was Marius Petipa, the French ballet master and choreographer for the Imperial Ballet in St. Petersburg, who first used the title in the 1890s when he bestowed it upon Italian virtuosa Pierina Legnani, a guest artist with the company, following her historic performance of *Cinderella*. Legnani astounded the audience in the *coda* of the *Grand Pas d'action* of the final act with a never before seen 32 fouettés *en tournant*. Less than a decade later, Mathilde Kschessinka was also given the same crowning title by Russia's Nicholas II. In the one hundred years since, only eight ballerinas in the world have been designated an *assoluta*; Alicia Markova (United Kingdom, 1933), Alicia Alonso (Cuba, 1959), Margot Fonteyn (United Kingdom, 1979),

Anneli Alhanko (Sweden, 1984), Phyllis Spira (South Africa, 1984) and Alessandra Ferri (Italy, 1992).

Plisetskaya danced onstage well into her 70s, a testament to her longevity and brio as a dancer, and continued performing challenging parts including the *Dying Swan*, the poignant *piece d'occasion* created by Fokine for Anna Pavlova which is done almost entirely *en pointe*, balanced on the toes, until the swan dies. She was still dancing the *Dying Swan* on tour with her company, the Imperial Russian Ballet, decades after most dancers retire from performing.

Plisetskaya's name opened many doors for the troupe of young dancers. Often in foreign countries following a performance, principal dancers, including Olga, would join the superstar and her friends at dinners with famous people and heads of state. This was an exciting time in Olga's life, to be in the company of and influenced by an icon. The two developed a close friendship that continues to this day, and said this:

"I will always remember Olga with her distinct individuality, her precision in movements with great intricacy, a union of heart and mind, a deep understanding of the roles she dances and great stage charisma and a sensitivity to music."

Following Olga's gold medal win at the Plisetskaya competition, she and the other winners were invited to a special ballet gala organized by Pierre Cardin in Paris in the spring of 1997. The event was held at L'Espace Pierre Cardin followed by a dinner at Maxim's, the fashionable Parisian gathering spot where thirty-six years earlier Plisetskaya visited for the first time.

For the gala, each dancer performed their winning work and Olga and Taranda once again showed *éclat* with their *Tango*. After the show, when Olga was introduced to Cardin, he graciously said, 'Oh, you did the *Tango*?' and complimented her on her fiery passionate portrayal. Courteously, he took Olga by the arm and escorted her into the reception area.

Being in Paris with Olga and her dance company, Plisetskaya must have remembered how she felt being introduced to the rich and famous of her day in the most romantic and exciting city in all of Western Europe. The ballet world of Paris embraced her, and it seemed years later, she wanted to share similar experiences as a mentor to young dancers. She wrote in her autobiography about borrowing the expensive couture of her close friend, Elsa Triolet, when she has occasion to meet the stylishly famous. She wore Triolet's white fur stole when she met actress Ingrid Bergman and a black mink-trimmed coat for her audience with Jacqueline Kennedy. This could have been on her mind when one evening back in Moscow following a performance, she presented Olga with a black, floor-length designer evening gown from her personal collection. The long-sleeve, wool blend dress had simple lines, a large ruffle stand-up collar and matching ruffles at the wrist. Olga was honored to receive such a treasured gift.

Something else cemented their friendship during a tour of Japan. The company opened its performance with Plisetskaya dancing the *Dying Swan* followed by *Le Corsaire* and the *Tango*. *Le Corsaire* is Petipa's and Sergeyev's ballet with glamorous costumes, slave girls, and plenty of bravura dancing from swashbuckling pirates. For the role of Medora the slave girl, Olga brought along a jeweled crown she had used for years playing the role. The sparkling headpiece is especially illuminating when Medora dances the famous *pas de deux* with Conrad. Olga sews her own costumes and tutus and has a collection of jeweled crowns she uses for various roles. A ballerina is always prepared with her own personally fitted tutus and tiaras. In Japan, the company rehearsed at a studio then, the following day, held dress rehearsal onstage with lighting and costumes.

For the special opening number, the cast presented Plisetskaya onstage. She wore a beautiful Pierre Cardin dress, then decided she needed a crown to complete her ensemble and asked to borrow Olga's. Excitedly, Olga ran to the dressing room and brought back her gold and bejeweled headpiece. Olga resumed her place onstage with the other company members, holding various positions lying down and on bended knee, behind Plisetskaya. The rehearsal went fine, but during the live performance something was missing.

"*I remember lying on the stage with the other dancers and when the music played and Maya did her first steps, the lights came up and we looked at her. I thought, 'Oh, my gosh.' I was ready to die. I realized she was without her crown. I forgot to bring her the crown. Later on, a friend of mine said, 'Don't worry. She's a real queen, she doesn't need the crown.'*"

CHAPTER 9

RISING STAR

FACING THE BIGGEST DECISION OF her career, Olga thought through the possibilities and the pros and cons of each. In the end, she turned down the contract with Northern Ballet. She wanted to stay in Moscow and continue her dance career just as she had planned. And she was still in love with Taranda and didn't want to leave.

She would eventually swallow a bitter pill when her relationship with Taranda crumbled. Rumors of his other girlfriends surfaced among her circle of friends, and she later discovered he was seeing another woman. The loss had to be devastating for her. She prefers not to talk about her past relationship with Taranda, but those around her knew the blow was crushing at the time.

She eventually left his ballet company and moved on with her life. This was a time of personal and professional transition. By 2000, her close friend and mentor Nina Osipyan had left Russia for a teaching career in New Zealand and eventually Australia. And Maya Plisetskaya too had parted ways with her company.

Instead of letting another lost love relationship ground her emotionally, Olga threw herself into her career. She was in search of a new coach, someone who could continue to inspire her in different ways as an artist. She had always wanted to work with Tatiana Popko, the legendary teacher and repetiteur at Moscow Classical Ballet and finally she had the opportunity. The company was known for catapulting the careers of many acclaimed dancers including Vladimir Malakhov, Irek Mukhamedov, and Galina Stepanenko among them.

Olga adored the company's classical repertoire and its busy touring schedule that would take her around the world. She also had the freedom to be a guest artist with other companies and perform at galas when invitations were extended, and they always were.

By now, she had become a bright star in Moscow and well known and respected in the Russian ballet world. She gained a reputation as a consummate artist who danced with a dynamism and esprit all her own. She delivered riveting performances, capturing the gentle dispair of *Giselle*, the bubbly grandeur of *Don Quixote's* Kitri and the sweetness and darkness of *Swan Lake's* main character Odette/Odile. She could be playful and ebullient and sultry and seductive. She could make each role her own with just the slightest nuance in her *port de bras* or the reach in her *épaulment* or a look with her eyes or the stretch of her neck. Her flexible back and beautifully arched feet set her apart from other talented ballerinas. Her musicality is as natural as her breathing. She knows how to carry the subtleties of drama without unintentionally forcing a performance. Her dancing comes from deep within the soul with all of its anguish and beauty.

As with all prima ballerinas, Olga's perfectionistic qualities continued to drive her to develop and push herself even further. Olga was never satisfied unless she was improving and was often overly critical of her work. Years later she looked back on that harsh voice inside her head with some regret. Her perfectionism drove her to break a customary practice in Russia; she didn't invite her former Bolshoi Academy teacher, Ludmila Nikonova, who had the most influence on her in school, to her professional performances. Each time Olga considered inviting Nikonova to a show, she was stricken with fear. She told herself she needed more practice, that she hadn't quite mastered the role, and her former teacher should not see her perform. She wanted Nikonova to see her at her best and she always felt she needed more rehearsal. She would invite her *next time*.

During her previous stint with Moscow Classical a few years earlier, Olga was a soloist. But now, she returned as a principal, a prima ballerina. The company's artistic directors for more than thirty years were the wife-and-husband team Natalia Kasatkina and Vladimir Vasilyov, widely known for their *Creation of the World*, made for the Kirov Ballet in 1971 and danced by Baryshnikov (as Adam) and Irina Kolpakova (as Eve). It was refreshing for Olga to tackle the lead female roles in their versions of *Romeo and Juliet*, *Spartacus*, *Creation of the World* and other ballets with the guidance from Popko.

Popko, who was married to the dancer Boris Akimov, was a quiet, petite woman with huge eyes who led company class every morning even well into her later years.

"Tatiana was a wonderful woman and an amazing teacher. She never pushed her dancers, she gave us the chance to develop the character ourselves, she guided us. She would sit in rehearsal in the studio very quietly and watched everything. She wouldn't give many corrections but when she did her words were profound. If after a performance she said, 'You did okay,' that meant it was really, really good."

Moscow Classical was a large company more financially stable than Imperial Russian Ballet with a vast repertoire of traditional three-act, Soviet-style ballets which required elaborate costumes and stage sets. By contrast, when Imperial Russian toured they performed mostly gala pieces in the typical *pas de deux* style.

Moscow Classical rehearsed in an historic building, the old former Bolshoi Ballet Academy across the street from the Bolshoi Theatre. "The dancers who passed through there left something almost palpable. You can feel it when you step inside. It feels like a temple of the arts." Every day, Olga took class with Popko in the old building. A black and white portrait of the late Naum Azarin-Messerer, from Russia's Messerer ballet dynasty, who was a teacher that greatly influenced Malahov among many other students, hung on the wall, massive and commanding. "In that picture, he seems to be looking at you," Olga says. "When you're in that old studio and Tatiana is in front of the class, you can't help but feel this great history with you."

CHAPTER 10

FROM CHINA WITH LOVE

WITH THE START OF THE new millennium, Olga felt as though she was starting another chapter in her life. With two failed marriages behind her and the break-up with Taranda in the past, at age thirty, she was hopeful about her future just as she's always been. She spent little time in the past wondering where she would be if she joined Northern Ballet and preferred to focus her energy on what lies ahead. She keeps most self-reflection to herself.

The year 2000 found her guest starred with the Russian National Ballet, a touring company based in Moscow without its own theater or studio space. As was common with relatively new theater companies, this one rented rehearsal and performance space. The company traveled extensively, favoring runs in Italy and China. On her second trip to China with the company, something magical and wondrous happened that would prove life changing in a way she could only have dreamed. Her own real life love story was about to unfold.

One morning when she walked into Russian National Ballet's company class, a young soloist, Yevgeny Anfinogenov, immediately recognized her from television. The ballet world is small in Moscow and everyone knew her. At once, he was struck by her beauty and physical presence. But, Genya, as he is called, was barely twenty-one and told himself, "Forget about that girl, just do your job and go home. She's a prima ballerina and you have no chance even to look at her."

Soon he became smitten and would exchange glances with her while pass-
ing in the studio. Still, he remained too scared to approach her. One day,
Olga and the troupe were rehearsing *Sleeping Beauty* and Genya was one of
the four cavaliers. During rehearsal of the beloved Rose Adagio sequence,
where the ballerina holds exquisite balances *en pointe* while holding the
hand of each suitor, he feared he would do something wrong. He didn't
want to embarrass himself in her presence. Olga remembers him as being
very patient as a partner and even then she could feel he was trying to do
his best.

When the company performed *Swan Lake*, Genya decided to do
something that would get her to notice him. He was so captivated by her,
he watched Olga during the second act when he wasn't dancing. Since Act
II requires only female dancers onstage, Odette and the female corps de
ballet, the male dancers typically took a smoke break on the step outside
the stage before returning for their parts in Act III. Genya stayed and
watched her every night. "She puts her soul into her dancing," he said.
"She opens her soul and you can read her like a book. There are only a few
ballerinas in the whole world who do this."

Olga noticed someone watching her in the wings but it was too dark
to see. Finally, someone in the company told her it was Genya. She was
surprised and thought it was a nice compliment.

About six months later, the company embarked on a two-month tour
of China during the winter. Inside the Beijing airport, Genya saw Olga
struggling to carry two cumbersome pieces of luggage and noticed no one
came to assist her. "I just offered to help her with the luggage and it was
the first time I talked to her," he recalled. Still, he was afraid to carry on a
conversation believing he had no chance with her. "In my head I thought,
'it's not going to happen.'"

On a break for a few days during the China tour, he and a friend were
sitting in the hotel lobby when Olga came breezing in from shopping at
a nearby market. That evening, the company's director invited the entire
troupe out to a local restaurant and nightclub. "I don't know how this
happened but she stopped in the lobby to say hello and I invited her to

the restaurant with everybody. She told me, 'Yes,' and would change her clothes and then be ready to go."

This was the couple's first unofficial date, and Genya fell head over heels. Right away, he was in love and had thoughts about marriage and a family even though he was young. She was far more reluctant and recognized their differences; she was older and he was a soloist, which is considered a lower rank than a principal. Still, she found herself thinking about Genya more and more.

"He was a very good person and right away I felt so safe and comfortable with him, I had a feeling like I was home, I was surprised about my feelings. I had that feeling that you just know it's right."

The next night the couple went out again and talked more and Olga started feeling she could spend her life with him. After just a few weeks, Genya asked her to marry him. She said *yes*. "It was love at first sight," she said with a giggle. "I woke up the next morning with that wonderful feeling in my heart."

For the next several weeks the couple was inseparable. After his performances and on days off, the couple explored China's cities, from Beijing to Shanghai to Xi'an, braving the cold and snowy winter. They strolled through Tiananmen Square and the Forbidden City holding hands. They marveled at the ancient traditional Chinese architecture. They explored quaint neighborhoods and enjoyed the local cuisine in cozy cafes. On the day the troupe visited the Great Wall in freezing temperatures, Olga came down with the flu so they both stayed behind at the hotel.

When the couple returned to Moscow, Olga shared the exciting news with her family and close friends that she and Genya were engaged. Needless to say, they were all shocked. Many of them told her she was crazy to marry him because he was younger and not on her level as a dancer. They worried this could be another mistake. They didn't think the marriage would last or that she would be happy. But Olga knew wholeheartedly this was the right choice. Genya was the one.

CHAPTER 11

DREAMS COME TRUE

SOME YEARS EARLIER, WHEN OLGA danced with the Imperial Russian Ballet, they company didn't have its own theater to call home. They bounced around performing in various local venues including the Stanislavsky Theatre, the Kremlin Theatre, and the New Opera Theatre, an opera house built in 1991 by its conductor Yevgeny Kolobov, who worked with many ballerinas over his career including Ekaterina Maximova. The ballet company also toured with the New Opera Symphony, and many of its guest directors got to know Olga.

One of those was Arthur Tsomaya, who called Olga in early 2002, saying he was now directing opera and ballets and wanted to collaborate with her on producing some evenings of dance in Moscow. While Tsomaya had a career outside of the arts, he was the president of Russia's now defunct Transeuropean Airlines, this would be his first foray into ballet production. His call to one of his favorite ballerinas with an irresistible offer not only proved mutually beneficial, but it would ultimately change the course of Olga's life and career dramatically.

Tsomaya invited Olga to create and star in an evening-length program that received as much advance publicity as any major production at the big-name theaters in the city. She would have the 700-seat New Opera Theatre for the evening, beautiful stage sets, a corps de ballet, a live orchestra, press coverage, and the chance to choose any Romantic ballet and the partner of her choice. This was a rare and delectable opportunity for a prima ballerina, and Olga was thrilled at the chance. First, she thought about what she wanted to perform, then she started dreaming of the perfect partner.

She decided on *Giselle* with Nikolai Tsiskaridze, the remarkably gifted Bolshoi star, whom she knew. Olga had partnered with him in *Sleeping Beauty* while on tour in Jerusalem in 1997. For that role, she prepared her Princess Aurora with another company member who stood in as the Prince until a day before the show when Tsiskaridze flew in. During the dress rehearsal, Olga revealed to him she never danced Aurora before and asked if he could he lend extra support onstage if necessary. He was shocked she hadn't danced the role previously as she delivered a flawless performance. "He helped me a lot," she remembered. "He could make a ballerina shine onstage."

Olga and Tsiskaridze's *Giselle* premiered in March 2002 and was a huge success, perhaps in part to a frenzy of advanced publicity throughout Moscow including large posters displayed downtown, in newspapers and magazines ads, and TV interviews with the stars.

The one person Olga wanted to invite see her dance in this performance was her former teacher Nikonova. While it's customary in Russia for dancers to invite their mentors to see them onstage, Olga never felt ready to have Nikonova watch her. Many times she considered inviting Nikonova, but the perfectionist inside her head talked her out of it. "It's not easy to let her see me unfinished. I always thought, this part could be better or that part could be better. I wanted her to see my best." This time, Olga felt ready for her teacher to see her in a most favorite role she danced so many times before. Olga asked Nikonova to come to the show, but her former teacher would be out of town and was unable to attend. This regret stayed with Olga throughout her professional career and grew deeper. Years later, Olga gained more of a perspective on it.

"When I was in Russia, I was so critical of myself. I didn't want Ludmilla to see me yet. I thought I was not ready. Then I left and she never saw me perform. When I came to the U.S., I started thinking that wasn't right. I'm more ready to invite her to see what kind of artist I am. Sometimes it's good to be a perfectionist and sometimes it's not."

With the *éclat* of the *Giselle* performance, Tsomaya started planning a second evening a few months later. This time, Olga considered dancing the highly-spirited and sexy role of Zobeide in *Scheherazade*. To play opposite her, she thought of Alexei Ratmansky, whom she danced with in *Giselle* while on tour a few years earlier. He had the right dramatic qualities and bravura to capture this role. But Ratmansky had stopped dancing to pursue his choreographic work and was already creating ballets for companies around the world. Since he wasn't performing anymore, he politely turned her down. With a *"no"* from Ratmansky, Olga reconsidered her plan.

As she explored whom to dance with, it occurred to her maybe this show wasn't solely about her. One of her favorite Bolshoi dancers, who had a terrific career and could deliver astounding performances in many of the classical male roles, wasn't even in Moscow anymore. Alexander Vetrov, who goes by Sasha, was a dancer of extraordinary range, and Olga saw him onstage in a variety of roles during her years with Grigorovich's Bolshoi troupe.

"When Sasha was a dancer at the Bolshoi, he was a very nice person. When an artist comes onstage, there's an aura around them. He had that aura. He's a good person, professional, classical, elegant, sometimes romantic, sometimes humorous. He stands out in my mind as the perfect Solor in La Bayadére. His body was great, his style was great for this ballet. At this period, he was the best dream dancer at the Bolshoi. I thought of Sasha. I realized it could be a big deal for all Russian dancers who knew him. Sasha was a huge star and he left Russia. He's a great dancer, and I thought he should dance again in Moscow, the audience needs him. I have to do this, it's not right that such a great dancer is not performing at home."

But by 2002, Vetrov had left the theater after a fall out with the new artistic staff in the years following Grigorovich's reign. He had moved to America with his family and was performing with regional ballet companies in the south.

When she called him, Vetrov enthusiastically accepted her offer to dance. But he had a suggestion. Why not do *Carmen* and also introduce

Russian audiences to *Bonjour Brel*, a neo-classical piece by choreographer Eddy Toussaint about two young lovers in Paris set to the music of Jacques Brel.

She was intrigued by his suggestion. A few years earlier, Olga had learned *Carmen* watching Plisetskaya rehearse the cast even though she didn't get to dance the whole ballet. The firey Spanish masterpiece, which first premiered at the Bolshoi Theatre in 1967, is set to music by Bizet and Rodion Shchedrin.

The pair settled on performing both works at the New Opera Theatre. When Vetrov arrived in Moscow for the performance in June 2002, he was stunned at the widespread media publicity given him and was elated being back in the spotlight. He must have felt a sense of redemption in a way coming back to dance after leaving his country and stardom for what turned out to be a more modest career in the U.S.

Vetrov was grateful to Olga for bringing him home to dance. Afterward, he asked her to consider moving to America and joining his new company. "If you want to try a new life and join my company," he told her, "I'd love to have you."

Intrigued by the idea of living in America, she considered Vetrov's offer for several months. She carefully played out in her head many times what life would be like in a new country. Although she visited many American cities on tour before, it was nothing like living there. Could she trade her name recognition in Moscow's ballet world for the unknown in the U.S.? Would she and Genya both continue successful careers in America? Was she ready to leave behind the negative things about living in Moscow including the extremely high cost of living and the ever-growing presence of terrorism? She spoke little English and was used to life in a big city. How would she take to living in a southern town?

Many things weighed on her mind about such a move. However, every time she told herself she would stay in Russia, the quiet voice inside her head remained unsettled.

Several weeks after her performance with Vetrov, Olga and Genya married on July 10, 2002 in an intimate morning ceremony. They kept their wedding small and hosted a breakfast afterward with family and close friends. Then, by mid-afternoon, the couple were at the airport catching a flight to Skopje, Macedonia with the Russian National Ballet where Genya would perform for two weeks. They managed to honeymoon in the former Yugoslav Republic during the tour, as Genya's performing schedule wasn't too demanding and allowed for rest and leisure. The couple had plenty of time to relax on their own, enjoy the sites of the region, walk along the lakeshore together, and explore the nightlife in the cities.

That winter, which brought the heaviest snowfall to Moscow in a century, left Olga ready for a change. She called Vetrov to talk about his offer. She was still intrigued about moving to America, but for her, this wasn't a leap, it was a *grande jeté* and she was unsure she was ready to fly. Sensing her hesitation, Vetrov had a suggestion. He would return the favor and bring Olga to his company as a guest artist where they could perform again *Bonjour Brel*. She could test the waters and see how she liked performing at this company and contemplate making the move.

In March 2003, Olga arrived in Texas to perform *Bonjour Brel* with Vetrov for the Arlington Ballet. The company was highly impressed by Olga's performance and an offer to join the company would soon follow.

But back at home, Olga continued with Moscow Classical Ballet, routinely performing the full repertoire including *Swan Lake, Giselle* and *Don Quixote*. The repetitiousness of performing these ballets left Olga weary and wanting new challenging repertoire. With *Swan Lake*, Olga adored the character of Odette/Odile and this had become her signature performance.

By the summer, a series of events would change the direction of her career and eventually lead her on a new path.

Terrorism attacks in Moscow took a personal toll on Olga as she became fearful working in the theater in light of the horrifying Nord-Ost siege. On Oct. 23, 2002, during a performance of the big budget Russian musical, *Nord-Ost*, Chechen rebels stormed the crowded theater taking hundreds of hostages and murdering hundreds. After a three-day standoff,

Russian forces pumped deadly gas into the building killing the rebels and 130 hostages.

The horrible incident struck close to home on two fronts, Olga and Genya had wanted to see the musical, and they worked in similar Moscow theaters. "After that, I was trying to avoid going to public places because a terrorist attack could happen anywhere."

Then in June 2003, Olga's mentor, the musical conductor Kolobov, died suddenly of a heart attack. The theater he built held a memorial service and hundreds of people turned out to pay their respects including Olga. The orchestra played, opera singers performed, and a recording of Kolobov's voice was broadcast over the sound system during the service, lending a surreal aspect to the pageantry. Olga was saddened by his death and remembered advice he once shared with her. "I felt like he supported me and respected me as a dancer. He said a real artist should be talented and honest, and that your talent is a gift from God. A true artist is always honest onstage. When I sat in the audience during the funeral, I thought about his words and pledged to him that I would always be honest onstage. It was my promise to him."

The next day she was scheduled to dance *Giselle* with Moscow Classical at the Stanislavsky and Nemirovich-Danchenko Musical Theatre, but Kolobov's death left her feeling completely empty. The funeral drained her emotionally. She performed the role so many times on stages around the world and knew *Giselle* demanded tremendous emotional energy. She was under contract and struggled over what to do. Just twenty-four hours earlier, she swore she would always deliver an honest performance onstage. But on this day, she had nothing inside to buoy or steady her. Still late in the afternoon, she got into costume and makeup and warmed up backstage. She heard the last gentle chime of the theater bell, which meant she had just enough time to lace up her pointe shoes and take her place. She felt like she had nothing to give the audience. Suddenly, she saw people starting to run from the building. Her husband, Genya, appeared, carrying her large dance bag, motioning to her to head for the door. A fire had started on the rooftop and the ushers were rushing people out of the theater. Everyone got out safely and the performance was cancelled. The theater was in ruins. The cause of the fire remains a mystery to this day.

This was an ironic miracle of sorts for Olga, who didn't have to dance and break her silent promise to Kolobov.

A few days after the fire, the director of Moscow Classical called the company together and announced their make-up performance for *Giselle* would be *Swan Lake* and it would be performed at the Bolshoi Theatre a few blocks from the destroyed Stanislavsky Theater. Olga would be cast as Odette/Odile.

In an instant, Olga's mind raced back to when she was a child and saw her first production of *Swan Lake* on that very stage. This was her dream. And as she wandered off in thought, she remembered as a young girl watching a TV documentary on Maris Liepa and hearing his story. His wish was to dance Prince Siegfried in *Swan Lake* for the Bolshoi Ballet. He wrote it on a piece of paper and tucked it inside a book. Years later, he found that tiny slip of paper after he had become a huge star and shared his story of his dream coming true. After she heard this, Olga, too, wanted to dance Odette/Odile on the Bolshoi stage and wrote it down on a small piece of paper and placed it in a book. Only Olga never forgot about her wish, which came true. She danced *Swan Lake* on the Bolshoi stage twenty-seven years later. This was her last performance in Moscow before moving to the U.S. Her performance would be the perfect end to her Russian career, and she could continue on without any regret to the next journey ahead.

CHAPTER 12

COMING TO AMERICA

BY THE END OF THE summer of 2003, Olga and Genya accepted Vetrov's offer to join Arlington Ballet as principal dancers and move to America. The new opportunity was exciting at this point in her career, and dancing new repertoire, specifically by George Balanchine, made it even more enticing.

"People say we lose all of the opportunities that we don't accept. In Russia, I already did my best. I prepared a lot of principal roles and worked with many different and wonderful companies. But my future there was more of the same. When Sasha offered for both of us to work at an American ballet company, we thought it could be very interesting. We knew we could always come back [to Russia] if we wanted. It was a pretty easy decision."

The couple moved to Arlington, Texas, in August and began rehearsing for the company's fall season. At Arlington Ballet, Olga worked with Vetrov and Paul Mejia, the former New York City Ballet dancer and Balanchine protégé who is the ex-husband of American ballerina Suzanne Farrell. Mejia also worked with the renowned choreographer Maurice Béjart. Mejia and Vetrov were co-artistic directors of the company and Vetrov's wife, Yelena Borisova, ran its affiliated ballet school. The company was thrilled an artist of Olga's stature would join their troupe. One of the company's board members, Sharon K. Nolan, called landing Olga "a real coup because she's such a high-caliber dancer."

In America, Olga expanded her repertoire with more neo-classical roles and modern works than she had danced before, and collaborating with Mejia was a natural fit. He coached her on some of Balanchine's most beloved works including *Apollo, Prodigal Son, Concerto Barocco,* and *The Four Temperaments,* as well as his own choreography which included the brilliant *Webern Pieces, Violin Concerto, Eight by Adler* and others. Mejia's training under Balanchine and respect for the Vaganova style meshed well with Olga's background and aesthetic.

"She's one of the unique ones, she's so versatile," Mejia said. *"She's still so rooted in the old world and can do the great classics so well, it's part of her soul. And she can do more modern work. She's still discovering, she's an eternal student. I love Olga's artistry and I respect her enormously. She's beautiful and she's got everything. She's so well-rounded and her work ethic is beyond reproach. She is one of my best memories in my career. She's probably the last great ballerina I've had a chance to work with. She's extremely special and she's brought me a lot of enjoyment."*

On her first day in the studio with Mejia, she learned her first Balanchine piece *Divertimento no.15* (1956), which is named for Mozart's masterful score. She found the steps comfortable and the piece musical and classical.

For her opening season with the ballet company, Olga planned to dance in two of the evening's offerings in *Divertimento no. 15* and the *Dying Swan,* but then something happened. The third piece on the program was a Mejia *pas de deux* called *Inspiration* set to classical guitar music. Mejia choreographed his Spanish-themed dance for Vetrov and guest ballerina Lucia Lacarra, who was with the San Francisco Ballet and later the Bayerische Staatsballett. But Lacarra backed out at the last minute and Mejia placed Olga in the lead. She would dance in all three of the evening's works.

Vetrov and Mejia developed Arlington Ballet into a company known for its classical Russian dancers. The repertoire was a harmonious mix of traditional and neo-classical with Vetrov restaging many traditional Soviet-style story ballets and Mejia bringing Balanchine and his own choreography. With its strong base of imported Russian dancers, the company had wide appeal in North Texas, cultivated a loyal audience, and consistently received glowing reviews. In 2004, Arlington Ballet changed its name to the Metropolitan Classical Ballet and they moved their performance space from the 2,700-seat Texas Hall Theater at the University of Texas at Arlington to the elegant Bass Performance Hall in the heart of downtown Fort Worth. Even though the Bass has fewer seats, 2,056, it feels like a grand classical European opera house. The company's rehearsal studios and ballet school remained in Arlington.

After Olga's first three-month season, the couple returned to Russia for a month-long break. Living abroad, at first, didn't feel much different than life in Moscow and being away on tour for two to three month stretches. But after a while, homesickness set in and she started feeling a mixture of emotions common to all émigrés; a disconnectedness from both their homeland and where they're at, a feeling of being somewhere in between and not belonging anywhere. There's a longing for home, a questioning of why they left and a strong feeling of unsettledness in their new land. Olga remains close to her parents and not seeing them regularly or having them at her Moscow performances was hard on her.

"The first few years were pretty difficult. Immigration is difficult even if you have lots of friends and a great job and friendly people around you. It's strange, my home is here but when I go back to Russia, I'm going back home, too. My city has changed because it's more developed, and I miss it. But I'm in the middle. We are Russian, we have a Russian soul, a Russian mentality and Russian roots. And now we have a Western-style life. We speak English. We still feel like we're Russian here but when we go back to Russia something feels different. The American life style is now normal for us."

Ratmansky perhaps described it best when he told an American journalist, "I have lost the feeling of home. When I am in Russia, I feel like I am a Westerner, and when I am in the West, I feel like a Russian."

In her newly adopted country, Olga continued working with the company's artistic directors on old classics and many new works. When they brought in Vladimir Vasiliev to coach the troupe in his *Les Promenades* (1978), Olga felt right at home. Vasiliev, a Bolshoi star who later became its artistic director, is considered a legend in Russia and one of the greatest male dancers of his era. He was married to Ekaterina Maximova and the pair immortalized the roles of Prince Albrecht and Giselle in *Giselle*. Vasiliev's *Les Promenades*, part of *These Charming Sounds*, is a plotless ballet he originally staged for the Bolshoi to serve as an alternative to the heavy, lavish Soviet-style productions for which the famed company was renowned. Back in Moscow, Olga worked in close proximity to Vasiliev when they both danced on the Bolshoi stage, she with Grigorovich's junior troupe. But it was only in the U.S. when the two worked together in *Les Promenades*, which is set to music by Jean-Philippe Rameau.

Working with Mejia allowed her to blossom even more artistically. He allowed her creative breathing room to fully explore new pieces on her own. The trust he showed reminded her of Tatiana Popko, who coached her at Moscow Classical Ballet in much the same fashion. "Paul gave me the freedom to do what I wanted with a piece of choreography really for the first time. He was the first choreographer to say, 'I'll show you the steps and surprise me. Dance it how you want.' He had complete confidence in me." He shared with her that Balanchine once wisely instructed him, "Never teach a Russian how to dance. They already have it in their blood."

She immediately took to Balanchine ballets and loved the role of Siren in *Prodigal Son*. One reviewer said her performance was "a marvel of deviousness preying on her victim," and compared her to the late Margot Fonteyn.

Olga also adored dancing Terpsichore in *Apollo* (1928), the muse of dance and song in the otherworldly tale of the young Greek mythological God of music. Balanchine considered this ballet his artistic coming of age, and it was the beginning of his collaboration with Igor Stravinsky in a partnership that would span the better part of the twentieth century. Balanchine first presented *Apollo* at age twenty-four with Serge Diaghilev's Ballets Russes in Paris. Although his 1979 revised and reduced *Apollo* is now widely danced by many companies around the world, Mejia chose to present the older, more significant version which he was familiar with as a New York City Ballet dancer in the 1960s. When Olga danced the role in

2006, Mejia called her portrayal spectacular and told her if Balanchine was alive, he'd be very happy with it.

In Mejia's eyes, Olga was the complete artist equally at home in classical and modern works. He was excited to see what she'd bring to each role.

"Everyday in rehearsal she showed me something new," he said. "Whatever you give her to do, she'll explore and find everything there is to find within it. She's secure in what she does. She's willing to be a student forever and explore, she's not afraid to try new things. When you get to that level of dancing, it's an equal partnership between dancer and choreographer. Your works are only as good as the dancers that produce them. Olga is limitless and can do it all. That's rare in many great artists and ballerinas."

Other choreographers such as Eddy Toussaint also recognized Olga's striking individuality and created works for her like *Edith Piaf*, his homage to the provocative, iconic French singer.

Part of Olga's appeal is her genuine warmth. She is without conceit or guile which is rare among world-class ballerinas. "A lot of dancers of her stature can be difficult to work with," Mejia said, "but she is a pleasure." It's common for dancers to behave badly toward each other because of the uber-competitive world of ballet. Mejia's wife, the former dancer Maria Terezia Balogh who taught at the ballet school, adores Olga and eagerly awaited seeing her rehearse new roles. "To me," Mejia said, "it's a testament of a great artist and it's so rare. Olga can cause jealousy and intrigue and people can be nasty."

Mejia was inspired to restage his own works for her, and he also entrusted her with a small piece of American ballet history. His *Scriabin Sonata*, set to the Russian composer's romantic *Sonata no. 3 in F# minor, Op. 23*, is about the ballerina. And when Olga danced the lead, surrounded by a corps of men, she wore a dress that once belonged to Suzanne Farrell, which Mejia had. The flowing dress, made for Farrell who is quite tall, was originally peach colored. But Mejia dyed it red for this ballet. Olga had the front skirt slightly altered to accommodate her smaller frame but otherwise it fit perfectly. Olga felt proud to wear the dress of one of America's great ballerinas.

Perhaps two of Mejia's most memorable works that Olga made stunning are *Violin Concerto* and *Webern Pieces*. He originally choreographed these two very different roles for his wife, Maria, years earlier and was inspired to set both of them on Olga, who elevated these characters with her emotional depth, crystalline artistry, and unmistakable brilliance.

Violin Concerto in D major, Op. 35 is set to Tchaikovsky's best-known and only concerto written for violin. The music is considered one of the most technically challenging violin works created. As a ballet, it required a lot of technical steps and non-stop movement. To learn the role, Olga first watched a DVD recording of Balogh's performance, then she was coached by Mejia. The adagio sequence, it turned out, was one of the most breathtaking Mejia had seen. As her favorite Mejia piece to dance, this role felt like second skin to Olga. And although she performed it only once, she dreams of reprising the role again someday.

In *Webern Pieces*, a duet for two, Olga and has performed it only with Genya and the couple were mesmerizing, their performance visceral and alluring. The modern piece is all about restraint and has none of the jumps and turns that devour a lot of open space. And with Anton Webern's sparse, atonal music that can sound flat, the work takes on a serious and sensual mood. It opens with Olga on a darkened stage standing below a single spotlight, dressed in a simple black leotard and tights. She stands in first position with her arms wrapping around her body. Genya is behind her, not visible at first. She moves with a feline grace and intensity. A slow leg raised to the ear captivated; the careful wrapping of each leg around the waist of her bare-chested partner proved powerfully intimate. The stunning end with an overhead lift of her tightly curled up quietly dazzled. The enormous appeal of the work was interpreting the choreography through her own ideas. She personalized the movements with her *élan*. Mejia designed the piece with the idea of giving something to the dancers who performed it knowing it would look completely different depending on the artist. Audiences today may not remember the work's interesting history. Mejia debuted it in 1986 when he was co-artistic director of

Chicago City Ballet with Maria Tallchief, the former New York City Ballet ballerina and ex-wife of Balanchine. It was a *piéce d'occasion* for the Jubilee Gala for the American Guild of Musical Artists and danced by Balogh and Joseph Malbrough. Later, when Balogh and Mejia came to Texas and were with the Fort Worth Ballet (which later became Metropolitan Classical Ballet), she reprised her role and was partnered by, of all people, Dallas Cowboy running back Herschel Walker. Bringing in the enormously popular NFL figure to partner a ballerina was an obvious stunt to draw young football fans to the theater. Who knows if it ever really worked, but the performance was noted in a *New York Times* review.

By 2006, North Texas audiences had fallen in love with Olga and she developed a loyal following. After performances, small crowds of young dance students and older ballet patrons waited with bouquets of roses backstage to present to her. Dance critics who followed the company consistently wrote so favorably about her that it often caused jealousy among other company principals whose performances didn't always meet with approval. "I feel alive when I dance and create," Olga said, "and if someone likes it and someone applauds or says something nice afterwards, I feel grateful. I tell them, 'Thank you for letting me know that you love it.'"

When it comes to dance critic reviews, her favorite one had little to do with her dancing. She glowed when one writer commented she looked skinny in a flesh tone, skin tight costume in the role of Eve in Vetrov's restaging of Kasatkina and Vasiliev's *Creation of the World*. This was a personal triumph for her remembering all those years during her Bolshoi training when teachers said she didn't look thin enough. So much was made about her muscular legs and how they didn't look right for the stage. Now as a prima ballerina, audiences view her the way she always wanted.

Her favorite classical role to perform is Nikiya, the beautiful temple dancer in *La Bayadére* which she first danced after coming to the U.S. Vetrov scaled down his version from Petipa's four-act ballet set in India, but the story nevertheless resounded. The beautiful temple dancer Nikiya is loved by two men, the kingly warrior, Solor, and the High

Brahmin. When her true love, Solor, must marry the Rajah's daughter, Gamzatti, she is heartbroken. After the scheming Gamzatti presents Nikiya with a flower basket that contains a deadly snake, Nikiya is bitten. Once she believes Solor and Gamzatti will be together forever, Nikiya refuses the poison antidote and dies. The grief-stricken Solor dreams of seeing Nikiya again in the Kingdom of the Shades but awakens and realizes he must marry Gamzatti. At the temple wedding, the gods intervene, everything is destroyed, and Nikiya and Solor are reunited in eternal love.

Rave reviews of her performances by the media didn't go unnoticed as she was named Best Ballerina by the *Dallas Fort Worth Weekly's Critics Choice* panel in 2007 and 2008 beating out the talented principle dancers at Dallas/Fort Worth's other highly-recognized ballet company, Texas Ballet Theater.

Olga found the company's repertoire wide-ranging and challenging and she poured everything she had into rehearsals. But she remained deeply disappointed about one aspect she was powerless to change; the troupe performed one-night-only shows with the seasonal exception of *The Nutcracker* which played multiple times. The financial constraints of running a small regional ballet company often didn't allow for repeat performances. This was difficult and different from Russia where she was used to performing back-to-back shows at longer engagements, which allowed her time onstage to perfect each character. "For me, it's much more useful to dance more onstage, you can develop the role and find more color and get better and better."

She also performed several lead roles for single-night engagements, something she never did in Russia. Trying to present full-length story ballets with a small company meant that Metropolitan Classical cut corps parts, but kept soloist and principal roles virtually intact in their full versions. That much dancing at one time is punishing on a dancer's body.

Eventually the stresses of working this new way and living in a different country caught up with Olga. Her life in America was strangely different;

her practice and rehearsal schedule changed dramatically, she was eating different foods and drinking different water than in Russia and her body reacted to the stresses. For the first time in her career, she dealt with injuries and experienced back pain.

While working under these constraints, she continued accepting invitations as a guest artist at galas and with other companies especially during the holiday season performing *The Nutcracker*, something she's always pursued throughout her career.

She also started teaching, something she had little time for earlier in her career. "The truth is when you have to survive and make money as a dancer you have to consider teaching," she said. She accepted offers to teach master classes with other regional ballet companies including the Tallahassee Ballet and student companies around the country. She found the work uplifting and enjoyable. Her friend and former partner, Dmitri Roudnev, asked her to teach a summer program for dance students and teachers at Buckman Performing Arts Center in Memphis, Tennessee. She sat in on Roudnev's class watching his coaching technique before it was her turn to instruct. She learned a few things from Roudnev that ultimately enhanced her own skills and possibly extended her longevity as a dancer. "He found the most correct way to explain the important rules to the students. If you explain them correctly, all of your students will be able to dance, even the less talented ones."

Olga continued focusing on the positive things about working and living in the U.S. including getting to partner with her husband. It was in America where the couple danced their first *pas de deux* together in *The Nutcracker*, she as the Sugar Plum Fairy and Genya as her Cavalier.

"Everything was special about it, he's my favorite partner. With Genya, onstage we breathe together because we think and feel the same way. No one partners me like he does. We work together on a piece for a long time, at the end of the day we discuss all the details at home. We continue to talk about it, we try something new or check something. He feels like me, he prepares his part the same way, he listens to music like me. We think absolutely the same way. We are a team, not just partners. It's not only about the steps, it's about many

different things. When I dance with him, whatever we do is my favorite. He knows exactly what I need onstage and I ask him about many small details. If it were someone else, they would think I'm very picky. Onstage, he gives me the absolute freedom."

CHAPTER 13
RAISON D'ERTE

LIFE IN AMERICA AFFORDED MANY more pleasures and comforts than in Moscow, where the exorbitant cost of apartments made owning one a nearly impossible dream.

After just a few years in the U.S., Olga and Genya were able to save enough and buy their first house in a Fort Worth suburb. Their ranch-style home has a pool and plenty of space for their two dogs, a mixed breed, Dasha, and a pit bull, Fedor.

Dancing is Olga's *raison d'etre* and she would like to continue for as long as possible. She travels often to perform and is sometimes away for long stretches of time. For this reason, the couple isn't planning on children. She is happy and content with her life, and she feels she can be a positive influence on youngsters through her teaching.

The couple lives comfortably in their home, which reflects her elegant taste and hard work ethic. Olga's style is a mixture of stately and modern with warm, rich tones. Her décor looks expensive but isn't because she did most of it herself; painted faux-finish walls, hand-sewed silky curtains and reupholstered furniture in rich-textured fabrics. They transformed the spare bedroom into a studio with a barre and mirror that Genya installed. Olga's personal collection of ornately detailed tutus and costumes from past performances that she has sewn over the years hang like artwork from long wooden spokes nailed high on the wall of their office, a storage idea she borrowed from the costume department of the Bolshoi Theatre. The couple's small yet functional kitchen suits them but has what would surprise most Americans, a mini-size refrigerator. You won't find caviar or champagne in their compact fridge, rather a few modest staples like a quart of milk and a half-dozen eggs. They firmly believe in living within their means and aren't caught up in acquiring worldly luxuries.

In 2009, Olga's parents visited the couple in Texas on their first trip outside of Russia. Since they don't speak English, Olga found herself translating for them and realized that her English was far better than she thought. Valentina and Alexander stood by their daughter throughout her academy years and her career, and they are immensely proud she realized her dream of becoming a prima ballerina.

With a place to call home and a stable life in America, Olga began re-examining her career. After several years with the Metropolitan Classical Ballet, she and Genya decided to part ways with the company in the summer of 2009 and she embarked on a career as a freelance artist. The small company eventually closed its doors and Vetrov moved back to Russia, where he rejoined the Bolshoi, this time as a coach working with principal dancers including American David Hallberg.

For the first time in her professional life, she wasn't attached to any one company. This left her feeling uneasy yet she knew the decision to leave was for the best. While she continued accepting invitations to dance as a guest artist and teach at various ballet schools, Olga searched for new experiences that allowed her to grow as a dancer. Breaking from a company was a gamble for her, especially living far from New York or other major cities where there is more opportunity for work for mid-career artists. She may have been worried at the outset, but her nerves were soon calmed.

In August 2009, the American *Dance Magazine* profiled the prima ballerina for the first time which helped elevate her status in the dance world and make her name known among dance aficionados everywhere. Then the British choreographer Christopher Wheeldon came to Dallas with his wildly popular ensemble Morphoses/The Wheeldon Company and her career took another turn.

Wheeldon is one of the most in-demand classical ballet choreographers working today with a flood of commissions from companies the world over. Many of his contemporary ballets, such as *Polyphonia*, *Liturgy*, and *After The Rain*, are performed around the globe, and he is just in his early 40s. In the world of ballet, where choreographers commonly can work well past their 80's if their health allows, 40 is relatively young.

In September 2009, Wheeldon arrived in Dallas for a two-week residency with his group and created a commissioned work that opened the Margot and Bill Winspear Opera House at the AT&T Performing Arts Center. Olga contacted Wheeldon before he arrived in Texas, and he invited her to take his company class and sit in on rehearsal. During class, Wheeldon immediately saw Olga's artistry and how it could enhance his ensemble of dancers. He offered her a contract to perform with his company during its 2010 winter season. Olga was excited to work with one of the brightest choreographers in the ballet world, who is known for his charm, effervescence, and intelligence.

Wheeldon's librettos are poetic and unexpected, dense and meaningful, and carried by thoughtful musicality. "He's positive and there's no pressure or anything negative working with him," Olga said. "It's a lot of fun. He respects each dancer for who they are. With his repertoire, I didn't have to force myself to get the steps, each movement was natural for me. Sometimes, you hear the music differently than the choreographer and you feel like a movement doesn't go with the music. In Christopher's work, I had no questions. He's very musical and we speak the same language. How he hears music was refreshing for me."

Olga joined his troupe for a month-long rehearsal in New York City before they toured in California and Canada. Stanford Lively Arts was one of many performing arts presenters that leapt at the opportunity to bring in Morphoses. Shortly after Lively Arts' Artistic and Executive Director Jenny Bilfield heard about Wheeldon's new company in 2007, she started plans to bring the hot new group to Northern California. Wheeldon's past work with the San Francisco Ballet made him a favorite among ballet audiences. Morphoses made its West Coast debut during a weeklong tour at several San Francisco Bay area venues including Stanford University's Memorial Auditorium, the Yerba Buena Center for the Arts, the Robert & Margrit Mondavi Center at the University of California, Davis and the University of California, Santa Barbara.

Olga performed in two of the three divertissements on the program, *Boléro* (2001), Alexei Ratmansky's fast-moving and contemporary take on Maurice Ravel's famous score, and Wheeldon's *Rhapsody Fantaisie* (2009) set to Rachmaninoff's piano music that was played live. *Rhapsody* was created for several couples and Olga partnered with Rory Hohenstein from the San Francisco Ballet.

"Rory is a great partner and I enjoyed dancing with him. He's a real artist and very musical, he has what all ballet dancers should have."

Dancing to live music, especially played by a gifted musician, is so inspiring that it makes a great dance performance even better. A month earlier at a gala event, Olga had one of the best dance performances of her career. She was an invited guest with Seattle Symphony's live orchestra at its Holiday Pops concert. The symphony welcomed an ensemble group of dancers, aerialists, jugglers, and mimes to perform onstage in front of the orchestra. Olga danced, under somewhat unusual conditions, the seldom seen *Russian Dance* from Tchaikovsky's *Swan Lake* which is set to beautiful music for solo violin and orchestra.

"I was in front of the musicians and I didn't have a lot of space to dance and it was slippery. But the quality of playing by the violinist (Tchaikovsky's music) was amazing. The violin in her arms came alive, and I had one of my best performances. I had almost no space in front of the musicians but I will remember this for the rest of my life because of the high quality of music."

With the other piece, Ratmansky's *Boléro*, Olga found it interesting dancing choreography created by her former partner. She was the only Russian in Morphoses who had danced with Ratmansky earlier in his career. Olga found his *Boléro* fast, fun, and freeing. The dance, which starts slow then gradually builds with Ravel's ebullient score, is about a competition among dancers. For effect, the couples have numbers on their bodices to approximate a contest. "It was fairly difficult technically, but you're pretty free onstage. To be able to do it nice, juicy, spicy, sometimes sexy, and act like it's a competition, you have to be physically ready so we rehearsed a lot. It was very fun to dance."

After the company's West Coast tour, they arrived in Ottawa, Canada to perform a one-night-only engagement, which closed its winter season. After the show, Wheeldon thanked Olga for joining his troupe and said it was a good experience for the other dancers to see her artistry.

Wheeldon, who is British, formed his company after leaving New York City Ballet. His vision was to make ballet more relevant to younger audiences by collaborating with leading artists and musicians and presenting at venues in New York and London, where he danced for a time with the Royal Ballet. He wanted to create a permanent company with a stable of great dancers hired with full-time contracts. Wheeldon handpicked top dancers from ballet's most elite companies, among them Darcey Bussell, Leann Benjamin, and Wendy Whelan. He also brought in freelance artists such as Drew Jacoby and Rubinald Pronk.

But the reality of trying to do it all, choreographing, teaching his repertory to an ever-changing group of dancers, running the business side of his company while searching for funding, proved too much for Wheeldon. In February 2010, after three years, he left his own company. Lourdes Lopez, Wheeldon's co-director, stayed and kept the name, and brought in guest choreographers in the 2011 season to drive the company forward. Eventually Lopez, a Balanchine ballerina, was hired away as the artistic director for the Miami City Ballet, where she's having great success reinventing that established company.

Olga was disappointed Wheeldon left the company. But she moved on, continuing to accept coaching jobs and guest artist parts.

Teaching has become a passion and she hopes one day to open her own school where she can develop students over time. For now, she is a master teacher at ballet schools including the Dallas Conservatory and the associate director of the Dallas Youth Ballet. She's an invited instructor at summer intensive programs including the Russian Classical Ballet Academy in Michigan. And some of her students are having success in the

Youth America Grand Prix competition, an international contest judged by representatives from the world's leading ballet companies offering scholarships as prizes. It was started by Larissa Saveliev and her husband, former American Ballet Theatre soloist Gennadi Saveliev, whom Olga knew in Russia.

"I try to give the students my best. I love to see their eyes sparkle when they feel like they learned something new. When I see small results, it makes me happy. It's an amazing feeling when you see a young dancer who wants to learn from you. They totally trust you. It's a lot of responsibility, and it's a lot of work, I have to be organized and prepare ahead of time."

One of Olga's teaching techniques is giving students examples of things to imagine while they are practicing steps. For example, when the Sugar Plum Fairy gingerly walks onstage in *The Nutcracker* before her variation, Olga tells the dancers to envision that it's winter and the floor is covered in ice. They must lightly walk across, gently touching the icy floor with their toes. "Immediately they feel it and move differently. That's acting and a dancer should act onstage all the time."

One joyful teaching experience came with a group of ten-and eleven-year-old students at the Tallahassee Ballet. Olga taught there in 2009 then returned for a second summer of instruction.

"I was very impressed, they are smart and they listen. They remembered what I told them a year ago. For me, it was a big deal. When I work with students, I have to be exact and every thing should be understandable, even though English is not my first language."

Olga's teaching process begins by first watching each student then determining the areas needing improvement. Musicality is critical in ballet and students must be able to feel the music and move correctly with the rhythm. She approaches teaching similarly to her former coach Tatiana Pavlovitch. It's critical to explain the artistry and logic behind the steps.

"Tatiana taught me never separate technique from art. If you only have technique, it's not ballet. She taught me to be honest onstage. Each movement should be more than just a step, it should have meaning and you can find it in the music."

Pavlovitch, who is now retired from teaching at the Bolshoi Ballet Academy, shares her thoughts about coaching. "Ballet is not a set of beautiful physical exercises," she said, speaking in Russian from her Moscow home. "It's a way of expressing complex emotional experiences as well as the specific characteristics of the roles. Ballet art is to appeal to the spectator's soul not just to please the eye."

She has watched Olga blossom from an eager young student into a world-class prima ballerina. Pavlovitch's perspective helps define Olga as a ballerina for our time.

"She is a dancer whose whole creative life has passed in front of my eyes. It was clear, at a glance, that Olga was a talented, passionate, and creative person in the way she learned and performed. She perpetually amazes me by the integrity of her path and the depth of her findings. She is self-sacrificing and obsessed. She is a rare person who remains committed to her creative principles despite the way to success today which is much shorter and more primitive."

Olga gives students valuable insight into a dancer's world and teaches them many things she's learned. Students mistakenly believe they should not dance in class but rather in rehearsal. That's incorrect, and Olga teaches her students how to show what they know during class routines. She also stresses that students must master basic concepts before tackling more advanced moves.

Pavlovitch also encourages students to work hard every day. If they do, they will continue to discover something new. This kind of advice is necessary to preserve traditional ballet, which she feels today is formal, elitist, and technocratic.

"When (Alexander) Pushkin, [the Russian poet], called ballet 'a soulful flight' he was right," Pavlovitch said. *"Olga carries on this tradition. Thanks to ballerinas like her, there is hope in my heart that ballet can be revived. Ballerinas like Olga must impart her knowledge and experience."*

Today, Olga's life is full between instructing aspiring ballerinas and performing in her adopted home state of Texas and many cities around the U.S. She and Genya return each summer to Russia where she continues to perform, most recently with the prima ballerina Uliana Lopatkina's touring group, the Anna Pavlova Gala. She has also tried her hand at producing and restaging a few ballets including Mejia's *Tchaikovsky Violin Concerto* in Moscow.

She has little time for outside interests let alone to reflect on how far her talent and unwavering determination has brought her. Sometimes, when she looks into the face of an eager young pupil who reminds her of herself, or catches a glimpse of one of her delicately jeweled tutus hanging in her home, Olga smiles privately at the remembrance of past performances. And then she will dream of the dances that are still to come.

DON'T STOP NOW

Watch many of Olga Pavlova's performances mentioned in this book at youtube.com and at pavlovaballet.com.

Take the next step and join readers from around the globe in the latest dance world news you won't find elsewhere and more. Sign up for our free email list at worldartstoday.com.

Made in the USA
Columbia, SC
09 December 2020